ARTEMIS

The Original Royal Princess

ANDREW SASSOLI-WALKER & SHARON POOLE

A selection of *Royal Princess* and *Artemis* luggage tags, 1999-2007.

First published 2010

Amberley Publishing
Cirencester Road, Chalford,
Stroud, Gloucestershire, GL6 8PE

www.amberleybooks.com

British Library Cataloguing in Publication Data.
A catalogue record for this book is available from the British Library.

ISBN 978-1-4456-0094-9

Typesetting and Origination by Amberley Publishing.
Printed in Great Britain.

CONTENTS

Captain Sarah Breton on the Bridge of *Artemis*, at Southampton, 13 June 2010. (*Andrew Sassoli-Walker*)

PREFACE

When I first joined P&O back in 1989, it was to *Royal Princess*, now *Artemis*, that I was sent as Third Officer. Over the next three and a half years, I rose through the ranks to both Second Officer and Navigator on board. I was next to return to her in 1996 as Safety Officer, and for the next two years I served both in that position and briefly as First Officer. In 2006 I joined again, this time for two years as Staff Captain, and have been lucky enough to complete the full list of ranks, returning here once more for my first command in April 2010. In total to date, some seven years of my life have been associated with this ship. She has taught me a huge amount and I have been lucky to sail with fantastic colleagues, many of whom are now good friends.

We shall miss her in our fleet.

Sarah Breton
Captain, MV *Artemis*
June 2010

The authors, Sharon Poole and Andrew Sassoli-Walker, with Captain Sarah Breton on the starboard bridge wing of *Artemis*, Southampton, 13 June 2010. (*Andrew Sassoli-Walker*)

FOREWORD

Let no one say a ship does not have a soul, or rather a personality; something intangible that you like or dislike, for no particular reason, regardless of actual sea-keeping abilities, handling or on-board facilities. If you like a person (or a ship) you forgive them their quirks and eccentricities. If you do not like a person (or a ship) then no amount of glitz, gloss or hype will change your mind.

When P&O Cruises announced the sale of *Artemis* in 2009, the news was met with the usual mixed reactions – in recent years she has frequently polarised opinion between those who felt *Artemis* was tired and dated and those who were dismayed at the loss of this unique ship to the British cruising public.

As a fourteen-year-old schoolboy in 1984, I (Andrew) was in awe of this beautiful vessel, which sailed into Southampton in November that year. She looked so futuristic when berthed next to the popular but by then aging SS *Canberra* (at twenty-three years, *Canberra* was nearly as old in relation to *Royal Princess* as *Artemis* is now to the new super-liner *Azura*), and ever since I have always enjoyed seeing her distinctive lines, and even more, being on board. Of all the ships that I (Sharon) have sailed on, *Artemis* remains a firm favourite and has given me many happy memories.

We both love the traditional aspects of cruising, and *Artemis* epitomises these, from the open teak decks to the single elegant dining room and intimate show lounges. *Artemis*' smaller size enables you to retain a connection with the natural world around you, whether she is gliding silently up a Norwegian fjord, sailing through the Straits of Gibraltar amid schools of dolphins, or through rain forest up the Amazon River. She was no production line vessel as are many of today's ships, but a one-off original whose like will not be built again. This book is our tribute to this beautiful vessel, the original *Royal Princess*.

Sharon Poole & Andrew Sassoli-Walker

Artemis, looking sternwards from the starboard bridge wing, 1 August 2010. When Bernard Warner joined *Royal Princess* as Chief Officer in 1984, he stood here with the new Deputy Captain, David Brown, and both commented on the awesome length of the ship. In comparison with other ships of that date, she was one of the largest afloat. (*Andrew Sassoli-Walker*)

INTRODUCTION

She is built to circle the globe and will, in her life, cross all of the oceans and touch many nations. In an age which presents mankind with a complex and demanding future, *Royal Princess* is representative of that fine thread of history from which progress is woven.

Jeffrey Sterling, Chairman, P&O, 1984

The motor vessel *Royal Princess*, named by HRH The Princess of Wales in 1984, inspired rave reviews from the outset with her sleek silhouette, elegant terraced stern, and wrap-around teak promenade deck; she soon attracted a loyal following among cruisers. Built at the beginning of the modern commercial age of cruising, she was the trend-setter of the cruise-ship world and holds a number of records, among them, the first contemporary cruise ship to have all outside cabins (the only other was the Nazi-built Strength-Through-Joy ship, *Robert Ley*), and recently, as *Artemis*, the first British passenger ship to be commanded by a female captain, Sarah Breton. At 45,000 gross tons, her size enables her to offer unusual itineraries and visit ports uncharted by the mega ships of today, but most of all it fosters a feeling of community, of family even, on board, not just among her ships' company, but also among the passengers.

Although some people disparage her for being older and for not having the facilities of the modern ships, what she does have in abundance is class and character, and it is clear that she is held in much affection by her crew. A ship is basically a metal hull full of machinery, and it is only as good as the men and women who run her; conversely, the ship also moulds the crew as it is they who have to work on her, live, and play on her. She may indeed have a few creaking joints and wrinkles, but this is not to say she does not remain a graceful, elegant lady.

The publicity of the time confirmed that *Royal Princess* was the largest and most advanced purpose-built luxury cruise ship ever conceived and constructed. Executive Purser Zak Coombs calls her 'The Little Ship with a Big Heart'. Small indeed by the standards of the 3,000+ passenger ships of today, but in her day one of the largest cruise ships afloat. Bernard Warner, currently Commodore of the Cunard fleet and Master of the *Queen Mary 2*, was at one time Chief Officer of *Royal Princess*. He remembers joining the ship with her new Deputy Captain, David Brown, in Helsinki: 'We both stood on the Bridge wing for the first time and looked aft. We both remarked on the length of the ship and its awesome size. A reflection perhaps on how quickly the ships grew larger with the Princess Sun class, followed by the Grand class and my most recent experience with *Queen Mary 2*.'

This is the story of *Royal Princess* and *Artemis*, with the memories of both passengers and crew and illustrated with many previously unpublished and specially taken photographs.

Royal Princess, approaching the Upper Swinging Ground at Southampton on another European summer's sailing, 1994. (*Andrew Sassoli-Walker*)

Artemis at anchor at Cannes, France. She is using her own companionway and tenders as well as a shore pontoon and tender to ferry passengers ashore, 10 May 2010. (*Sharon Poole*)

CHAPTER 1

PRINCESS CRUISES AND P&O CRUISES

Now one of the best-known names in cruising, Princess Cruises was established in 1965 by American Stanley B. McDonald. He began by operating US-based itineraries with just one chartered ship, the *Princess Patricia*. Today they have grown to become the third largest cruise line in the world, with a fleet of seventeen ships.

The first cruise offered by the *Princess Patricia* was from Los Angeles to the Mexican Riviera. Despite a reasonable season, the ship was not a great success, mainly because she had been designed for Canadian Pacific Railways' coastal service between Vancouver and Skagway and Juneau in Alaska, and thus had no air conditioning. She did, however, leave a lasting legacy in that the name Princess Cruises was chosen for the new company. Macdonald started to look around for something more suitable for his mainly west-coast clientele. The answer lay in the *Italia*. She was launched in 1965, and was one of the first modern ships built specifically for cruising. The original builders and owner had gone bankrupt, so the ship was in the ownership of a bank when she was chartered to Princess. At just over 12,000 tons and carrying approximately 600 passengers, she was a success from the start. Like the *Princess Patricia*, the *Princess Italia* began with Mexican Riviera Cruises (a marketing term coined by Princess in its early days), but was also used on cruises from San Francisco to Alaska. Three years later, this charter too was cancelled and the *Princess Italia* was repositioned in Europe under charter to Costa Cruise Line, while in return Costa's *Carla C* went to Princess. She was duly renamed *Princess Carla* to keep the brand identity. This became the first of the Princess ships to bear the Seawitch logo that was introduced in 1968. It was while working on the *Princess Carla* as the first ever female cruise director that Jeraldine Saunders

wrote the early chapters of *The Love Boat*. In 1975, this was adapted into a popular television series, running for several seasons, and is credited as being largely responsible for reviving interest, especially among younger people, in cruising as a holiday. In 1968, Princess Cruises was sold to Boise Cascade, although Stanley Macdonald bought the company back two years later, the year the *Princess Carla* was returned to her owners. The two ships that featured heavily in *The Love Boat* series were built in 1971 at Nordseewerke at Emden, Germany, for Flagship Cruises. Originally named *Sea Venture* and *Island Venture*, they were bought for Princess in 1972 and 1974 respectively, and renamed *Island Princess* and *Pacific Princess*.

In 1974, the Peninsular & Oriental Steam Navigation Company (P&O) acquired Princess Cruises. P&O were by then the world's largest shipping company with 320 ocean-going vessels of all kinds, from ferries and liners to container ships and bulk carriers. Their main passenger business was in moving people out to India and Australia, Britain's former colonies, but they had also been offering Mediterranean cruises (for first class passengers only) since the nineteenth century, diverting liners on the Australia route to cruising during periods when normal business was slack. Additionally, their ships carried mail, but as the use of air transport became more wide-spread after the Second World War, it was clear that P&O could no longer rely on mail contracts to subsidise line voyages. Passenger numbers were also reducing as air travel gained a market share and, following India's Independence, fewer civil servants and army personnel were being posted to the Subcontinent. Cruising however, was growing in popularity. To increase passenger numbers, P&O abolished the class separations on board, and began to expand into the

Sea Princess (left) passes *Pacific Princess* at the entrance to Southampton Water, 1994. *Sea Princess* was arriving back home after a refit while *Pacific Princess* was sailing on another European cruise. *Sea Princess* was sailing for P&O Cruises at this time, hence her buff funnel. The confusion caused by her anachronistic name was the reason P&O Cruises renamed her *Victoria* in April 1995. (*Andrew Sassoli-Walker*)

lucrative American cruise market. However, this plan suffered a major setback when, in 1969, there was an outbreak of typhoid on the *Oronsay*. This taught P&O an important lesson that the expectations of the cruising public were much higher than those of a person booking passage to Australia and all points east; the older ships fell far short of these standards, particularly those expected by West-Coast Americans. Five ships – *Iberia, Orcades, Oronsay, Orsova* and *Himalaya* (all built as ocean liners between 1948 and 1954) were sent to the scrap yard in quick succession. The loss of these vessels left a large gap that was filled perfectly by the acquisition of Princess Cruises.

P&O's 1972 *Spirit of London* (originally to have been Norwegian Cruise Line's *Seaward* until NCL pulled out of the deal due to price rises) was transferred to the Princess fleet, becoming the first *Sun Princess*. A further addition to the Princess fleet was the former Swedish transatlantic liner *Kungsholm*, purchased by P&O from Flagship Cruises in 1978, and then restyled and rebuilt in Bremen as the *Sea Princess*. She was initially based in Australia as a P&O ship until 1981, when her role there was taken over by the original *Oriana*. After that, *Sea Princess* alternated between P&O and Princess colours as she moved between fleets (this necessitated repainting her funnel each time – buff for P&O, white with the Seawitch logo for Princess!). The *Sea Princess* returned to the P&O UK fleet permanently and in April 1995 was renamed *Victoria*. This freed up the *Sea Princess* name to be used on a new Princess ship in due course, and differentiated between the two sister brands. Rather confusingly, the new *Sea Princess* became *Adonia* for P&O Cruises, then back to *Sea Princess* when Carnival took over the two brands and shuffled round the ships within the two fleets!

Royal Princess (right) berthed at Southampton behind *Sea Princess, 1994. Sea Princess* was originally Swedish America Line's *Kungsholm*, before being bought by P&O in 1978 and converted for cruising. It was then that her forward funnel was removed giving her a slightly off-balance appearance! She was based in Australia until 1981, after which she alternated between the P&O and Princess fleets before being permanently transferred to P&O Cruises and in 1995 renamed *Victoria*. P&O sold her in 2002 to Leonardo Shipping. At the time of writing, she is sailing as *Mona Lisa* under charter to Lord Nelson Seereisen. When this charter ends in August 2010, her future is uncertain, although it is rumoured she may become a tourist attraction in Gothenburg, Sweden, or possibly student accommodation in Stockholm. (*Andrew Sassoli-Walker*)

Left: Advertisement for *Royal Princess*' first European season of cruises, *Cruise Travel* magazine, October 1988. (*Princess Cruises*)

Above: Royal Princess, dressed overall at the London International Cruise Terminal, Tilbury, 1992. Note that one of the lifeboats has been lowered to embarkation level on the Promenade Deck for maintenance or a crew drill. The P&O house flag is flying from the jackstaff. (*Andrew Sassoli-Walker*)

Following their acquisition of Princess Cruises, P&O began to make plans to build a new cruise liner, specifically designed for the North American market. It was this ship that was to be launched as *Royal Princess* in 1984 and turn traditional cruise ship design on its head, setting the standard for all future ships to match – or beat! In September 1988, P&O also purchased the Monaco-based Sitmar Cruises, transferring all of its major tonnage to Princess, including three cruise ships then under construction. These became the *Crown*, *Regal* and *Star Princesses*. Along with ex-Cunarders *Dawn Princess* and *Fair Princess* it brought the fleet up to ten deluxe cruise liners. In these moves, P&O had not only removed their main competitors on the US West Coast operations, but had become one of the world's largest operators of cruise ships.

Always keen on innovation (it was Princess who introduced the concept of the one- or two-night Party Cruise), Princess ships became known for what was then the ultimate luxury – the private balcony – something taken for granted by many of today's passengers. Previously only available in the most exclusive suites, Princess ships offered the highest percentage of balcony cabins across all categories. Of *Royal Princess*' 600 staterooms, 152 had private balconies.

As Princess Cruises grew, so did their itineraries. In 1985, for the first time a Princess ship – *Pacific Princess* – was repositioned to the Mediterranean for summer and autumn cruises from Naples, Athens or Lisbon. This proved so popular that by the late 1980s they repositioned two ships, the original 'Love Boats', *Pacific Princess* and *Island Princess*, for summer cruising in Northern Europe. Their

Streamers are thrown by passengers as the band play for another departure for *Royal Princess* from Tilbury, 1992. (*Andrew Sassoli-Walker*)

new home port was Tilbury. This had been P&O's original home port for their line voyages until 1960, when *Canberra* and the original *Oriana* entered the fleet and were too large for Tilbury Docks. Although twenty-two miles from Tower Bridge, Tilbury is situated within the Port of London and was ideally positioned for access to the North Sea. The regular programme then became Mediterranean cruises in the spring, sailing from Barcelona, then Northern Europe itineraries from Tilbury before a transatlantic crossing back to the eastern seaboard of the USA for autumn cruises up the coasts of New England and Canada.

The 150th Anniversary of P&O in 1987 saw *Pacific Princess* represent the company at a lavish celebration alongside Greenwich in London. At that time, she was the only passenger ship in the fleet small enough to get that far up the River Thames. Two years later, *Royal Princess* also made her European debut when she was repositioned at Tilbury for some summer seasons.

In the 1990s, Princess altered their itineraries slightly to include calls in France, initially at Calais, then later Le Havre, so that American passengers could visit Paris. When Le Havre was introduced, *Royal Princess* made a popular return to the Hampshire port of Southampton, which became her UK home port from 1993.

In 1996, a new cruise terminal was built in Dover on the former Marine Railway Station site, at which time Princess Cruises moved their departures along the coast to the port, famous for its white cliffs. This changed again in 2000 when P&O signed a long-term agreement with Southampton. Shortly after this, the cruising arm of P&O was separated from the rest of the group to become P&O Princess. At this point, P&O Princess became a tempting takeover target and when a potential merger with Royal Caribbean Lines failed, the industry giant Carnival stepped in. On 17 April 2003, shareholders of both companies approved the merger and P&O Princess was purchased by the Carnival Corporation to form the world's largest cruise operating company in a deal worth US$5.4 billion. P&O Princess joined eleven sister brands, including Holland America Line, Cunard and the then newly formed Ocean Village. There were fears as to what would happen to the staunchly UK brand of P&O under the wing of the US-owned Carnival, but as had happened previously with Cunard, both P&O Cruises and Princess were kept as discrete brands. Aside from any other consideration, this made good commercial sense as they each offered a distinctive cruise experience, appealing to a different passenger base.

With Cunard no longer a competitor, there was a shuffle round of ships within the group. Cunard's *Queen Victoria*, then under construction, was transferred to P&O Cruises to become the third *Arcadia*, while Cunard were re-allocated a slightly longer and heavier version of the same Vista-class hull for later delivery. In 2005, to add capacity to Princess Cruises (especially in

Above: Royal Princess, dressed overall on her first visit to Southampton since her naming ceremony in 1984. She was about to sail on the first of another European season of cruises, 1993. (*Andrew Sassoli-Walker*)

Left: Royal Princess leaving at sunset in 1993, on her first Southampton departure since being named there nine years previously. (*Andrew Sassoli-Walker*)

P&O's two ships for adult passengers only – *Artemis* and *Arcadia* – in Southampton, July 2006. The cruise industry has changed greatly over the twenty-one years between the building of these two ships. Whereas *Artemis* is a unique and original design, *Arcadia* is one of the Fincantieri Vista Class of cruise ship, designed to span several brands within the Carnival Corporation. Other Vista Class ships include Cunard's *Queen Victoria* (albeit slightly modified) and Holland America Line's *Westerdam*. (*Andrew Sassolli-Walker*)

Europe in a bid to target UK passengers for this international company), one of P&O Cruises' 'White Sisters', *Adonia*, was transferred to them and returned to her original name of *Sea Princess*. This allowed them to compete head-on with Royal Caribbean Cruises International, who along with their Celebrity brand, were increasing their market share of British cruisers. In exchange for *Adonia*, the decision was made to move *Royal Princess* over to P&O Cruises. This allowed them to offer a wider choice of ship since, after the sale of the much-loved *Victoria* in 2003, there had been no vessel smaller than the new *Oriana* at 69,000 gross tons. *Royal Princess* was renamed *Artemis* and joined the then new *Arcadia* as an exclusively adult ship.

Cruising today is enjoying a popularity undreamt of in the early days. A study commissioned by P&O Cruises earlier this year revealed that cruises, once considered the preserve of the rich, are now more accessible than ever

before. Princess Cruises operates a fleet of seventeen ships sailing to all seven continents and carrying 1.3 million passengers a year. P&O Cruises have one of the younger fleets in the business, operating seven ships from 45,000 up to 115,000 tons.

At the time of writing, it feels like a new ship is announced nearly every month, with three major launches in 2010 alone – Celebrity's Solstice class *Eclipse*, P&O Cruises' 115,000 ton super-liner *Azura*, both launched in April, and Cunard's replacement for *QE2*, the *Queen Elizabeth*, due (at time of writing) to launch in October 2010.

The technological innovations and far-sightedness of the architects and designers of *Royal Princess* have left a lasting legacy in today's cruise ships, and while they may be nearly three times her size, many of the amenities and construction techniques were pioneered on this one ship.

CHAPTER 2

DESIGN AND CONSTRUCTION

I want to take this opportunity to thank the board of P&O Steam Navigation Company for the confidence they have shown in placing this outstanding order with our company. We believe the experience obtained by us during the construction of many previous cruise liners, together with the vast operational knowledge of P&O, has resulted in one of the most advanced purpose-built cruise ships ever built.

Tankmar Horn, Chairman, OY Wärtsilä AB, Helsinki, 1982

Royal Princess was the first P&O ship built for the company since the *Canberra* (1961) and the first cruise ship ever built for Princess Cruises. At just under 45,000 gross tons with a beam of 29.2 metres (95 feet) and a length of 232 metres (761 feet), she would be one of the largest cruise ships afloat at the time, just slightly bigger than the *Canberra* (*Queen Elizabeth 2* was larger, but was built and still then operating as a transatlantic liner). P&O traditionally expected a life span of twenty to thirty years from their ships so, from the very beginning, *Royal Princess* was planned as a ship for the twenty-first century. For this reason, rather than going for the easy option of an orthodox design, P&O wanted an imaginative leap forward both in style and technology.

The contract to build Hull 464, signed on 20 April 1982, was awarded to the Finnish firm of Wärtsilä, the largest constructor of luxury cruise ships in the world at that time, in the year of their 150th anniversary. Wärtsilä had delivered over fifty innovative designs in the previous ten years; an impressive third of all cruise ships built in that period. It included *Song of*

Norway (currently sailing as *Ocean Pearl*), *Nordic Prince* (currently sailing as *Aquamarine*), and *Sun Viking* (now the casino ship *Long Jie*). No British shipyard could compete on price, delivery date or design. Common to all earlier Wärtsilä designs was a sharply raked clipper bow, as seen on the *Nordic Prince*, although by the 1980s this had been slightly modified to the straighter profile seen on *Royal Princess*. This added more strength to the hull, particularly important for transatlantic crossings. Other Wärtsilä signatures were a lido deck with curving glass screen and a circular lounge built round the base of the funnel. The elegant horseshoe-shaped tiered stern was another outstanding feature, and a number of ships have followed this design, most noticeably P&O Cruises' current classic ships, *Oriana* and *Aurora*, both built at the Meyer Werft yard in Germany and the last ships built for them before they were taken over by the Carnival Corporation.

The final design for *Royal Princess* was the culmination of the work of many people; close to one hundred project consultants were employed to bring P&O's vision for this ship to life. The Wärtsilä research and design team under Kai Levander had been in talks with P&O's planning and technical staff for close on ten years prior to the official contract being signed. They worked together with the Danish firm of marine and naval architects, Knud E. Hansen, A/S of Copenhagen, who were also employed in a consultancy role on the initial technical design. Everyone, together with P&O engineers and technical experts, had to come to an agreement, not only on what was necessary and desirable, but also on what was practical. A model of the proposed hull was made so that wind tunnel smoke tests could be carried out on the funnel design. Senior P&O captains practiced handling the ship on a

Right: One of the two Wärtsilä builder's plates. This is the stern plate, affixed to the superstructure over the skylight to what is now the Wedding Chapel. The other is situated on the bulkhead at the bow on the Promenade Deck. (*Andrew Sassoli-Walker*)

Below left: Sixteen years of cruise ship design separates these ships – *Aurora* and *Royal Princess* – berthed bow to bow at Southampton's Mayflower Cruise Terminal in 2003. Already the growing size of cruise ships is evident here with *Royal Princess*, once the largest cruise ship afloat at 45,000 tons, just two-thirds the size of *Aurora* at 76,000 tons. (*Andrew Sassoli-Walker*)

Below right: The central crew walkway through the ship on Deck One, referred to colloquially on board as the 'Green Mile' or 'M1'. This allows most ship business to be conducted away from and out of sight of the passenger areas. Dedicated stairways link this corridor to a similar one on Deck Zero. (*Andrew Sassoli-Walker*)

Left: Hull 464 under construction in Wärtsilä's yard, Helsinki, 1983. The view is from the bow looking aft. It shows the pre-fabricated cabin sections being assembled above the public room decks. In the centre, an air-conditioning plant is being installed. The length of the ship filled this massive covered dry dock so the final tip of the bow had to be welded on once the ship was afloat and could be moved astern to allow sufficient space to do the work. (Southern Daily Echo)

Below: General Arrangement plan. This is one of the original builder's plans from the Wärtsilä Shipyard. It is framed on the wall outside the Chief Engineer's office on board. (*Andrew Sassoli-Walker*)

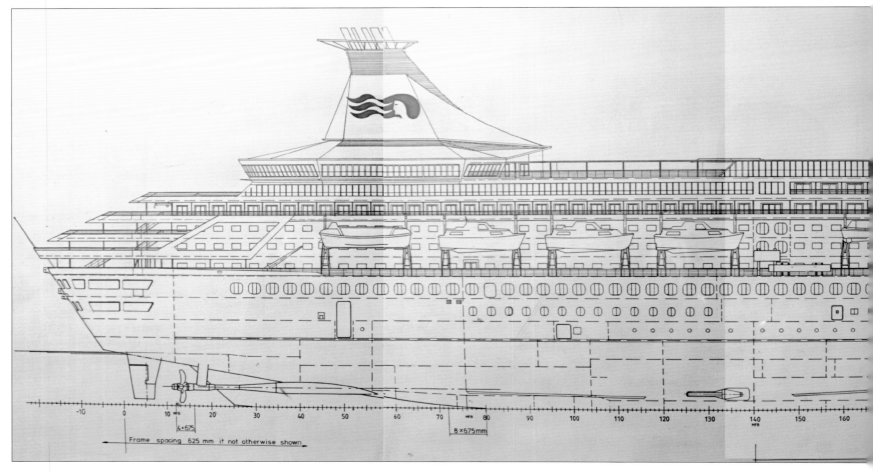

Frame spacing 625 mm if not otherwise shown

computer simulator, particularly concentrating on manoeuvring her in the US West Coast ports *Royal Princess* would spend much of her time visiting. There was even a model of the swimming pool made to test the effects of rough seas on the water in the pool. Full scale mock-ups of passenger cabins were constructed to try out different furnishings, lamps, tables and chairs sent by various manufacturers.

The end result was revolutionary for its time. Not only did all 600 staterooms have a view of the sea from a big picture window (the only portholes on this ship were in the crew quarters and medical centre on the two lowest decks), but also, aside from the Festival Theatre and atrium, every passenger space also had an outside view. This was achieved by building the public rooms under the main accommodation decks. Until that time, it

was more usual for the dining rooms, lounges and theatres to be high up in the ship, over the majority of the passenger cabins. Additionally, placing the staterooms to the outside of the hull allowed a corridor to run through the centre of the vessel (colloquially referred to on board as the M1 or the Green Mile as the floor is painted green) and meant all the maintenance areas – air conditioning, wiring, pipe ducts, lifts, service stores and pantries – could be accessed without disturbing passengers.

Construction began on 12 May 1983. The British Ambassador to Finland, Alan Brooke Turner began proceedings with the traditional laying of coins in the dock under the keel as an ancient symbol of good fortune and safe travels; this was most probably the first time the then new British one pound coin had been used in this way. The ship was to be built in a covered dry dock in the

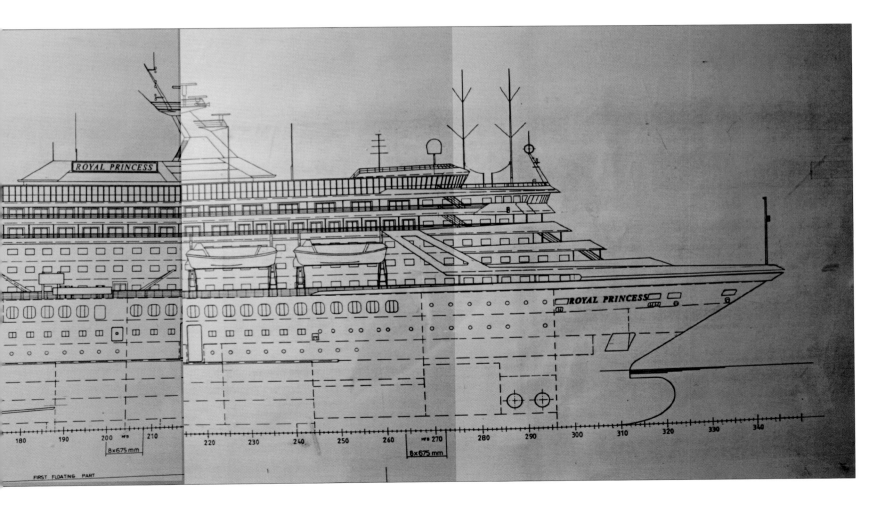

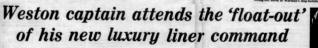

Wärtsilä shipyard in Helsinki, now part of the massive STX Europe group. At 240 metres (787 feet) long, this was, at the time, the largest enclosed dry dock in the world, but even so, with the ship at 232 metres (761 feet) long, the final tip of the bow had to be added after she was floated out. From the keel-laying onwards, up to 2,000 shipyard employees worked seven days a week to complete the ship in just two and a half years, managing to finally deliver her a day ahead of schedule!

The method employed to build Hull 464 was the now commonplace one of assembling prefabricated units. Steel was prepared in sections of up to 300 tons, blasted clean, painted under controlled temperatures and then transferred to the dry dock for assembly. Around 200 of these units were built, in some cases being pre-fitted with machinery and pipe work before being put together. A similar method was used for the bathrooms, which were manufactured on a production line before being transferred to the yard.

In June 1983, P&O made the announcement that the ship was to be named *Royal Princess* by HRH The Princess of Wales. On 17 February 1984, the dry dock was flooded and *Royal Princess* was edged astern to allow the final tip of the bow to be welded on in an overnight operation before the ship was floated out. The following day, four ice-breaking tugs gently eased *Royal Princess* out stern first into glorious sunshine and a harbour covered with 1 foot of ice! Despite the fact that her funnel was not yet fitted, there was just 1 metre (3 feet) clearance above her superstructure and 2 metres (6½ feet) either side, as the tugs pulled her out and turned her round to take her to the newly built £12 million fitting-out terminal. A short ceremony was conducted in the frozen harbour, when warm sea water from Southampton Water, flown out especially for the occasion, was poured over the bow to wish the ship good luck. From that early stage, *Royal Princess* would be linked with the Hampshire port, even if her home for the foreseeable future was to be in the USA.

It took another eight months for the ship to be completed. The concept for the interiors of *Royal Princess* was developed by the Los Angeles-based design consultants Hirsch Bedner. They, together with Njal Eide, the Norwegian architect appointed to head the project, were responsible for producing a

Top: *Royal Princess* being towed from the building shed to the new £12 million fitting out terminal through the ice-filled harbour of Helsinki, February 1984. Her future master, Captain John Young, was present at a small ceremony which was held to mark her Float-Out, at which her bow was splashed with warm sea-water from Southampton Water flown out especially for the occasion. (Southern Daily Echo)

Left: Article in the local newspaper from Captain Young's home town, Weston-super-Mare, Somerset, reporting his attendance at the Float-Out ceremony, 23 March 1984. (The Weston Mercury)

style and ambiance to appeal to the North American market, which would provide the main passenger base. 'Having worked with cruise ships for more than twenty years as an architect and interior designer, not one of the past projects has given me more professional and personal satisfaction than the splendid task of designing in total the interior of the most luxurious ship in the world, *Royal Princess* … this ship was to represent a new era in cruise liners, and traditional cruise ship design was in the process of becoming history', commented Njal Eide on completion of the ship. The aim was to create a simple elegant atmosphere, such as might be found in a top international resort hotel. As Michael Bedner of Hirsch Bedner & Associates put it at the time, 'When guests enter a hotel or embark on a cruise ship, they become actors on a stage. A transformation occurs when people walk into a great space. They respond to it and it makes them feel good. They become aware of themselves, their surroundings and other people in the space. The guest should be the actor and the audience simultaneously.' The emphasis was on neutral colours as a background to show off the furnishings, art and live plants. Darker accents in teak and brass, together with contrasts of texture, gave a stylish finish; for example the Reception Desk of polished fossil stone next to highly polished stainless steel. Subtle lighting and specially commissioned artworks

(for which £¼ million was allocated alone) provided the finishing touches so that, when completed, the ship would be the leader in design, innovation and elegance. There were four pools and two freshwater whirlpools. Every passenger stateroom had bathrooms with baths as well as showers, the showers having one fixed head as well as a hand-held one. Every cabin also had a multi-channel television, a refrigerator and individual climate-controlled air conditioning. Commodore John Wacher, an experienced semi-retired P&O captain, was involved in an advisory capacity in the design of the ship, and had quite a dilemma on his hands as he disagreed with the idea of every stateroom having a television. He was old school, and liked the convivial atmosphere created when people met and mingled with other passengers in public areas. He considered them part of the shipboard community and didn't approve of them hiding away in their cabins!

Passenger accommodation consisted of two Royal suites, twelve suites, two special deluxe staterooms and 534 twin outside staterooms, of which 152 had private balconies, or verandahs as they were called at the time, and the remainder a large picture window. In total there were nearly 1,486 square metres (16,000 square feet) of glass. The ship was also unique at the time for the ability to configure stateroom sleeping arrangements as either twin beds

Above left: Royal Princess awaiting top-coat painting while in her fitting-out berth in Wärtsilä's yard in Helsinki, June 1984. Note the painted out letter A in her name – did someone make a mistake? (*Alan Mackenzie*)

Above right: Royal Princess at the fitting out terminal in Helsinki, June 1984. There is a considerable amount of top-coat painting still to be done here, but she is taking shape. (*Author's Collection*)

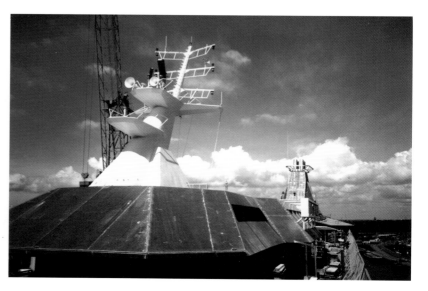

Above left: Royal Princess alongside in her fitting-out berth in Wärtsilä's yard, Helsinki, June 1984. The Horizon Lounge windows are being fitted and the Princess Cruises Seawitch logo is being mounted on the funnel. (*Alan Mackenzie*)

Above right: The roof of the Health and Beauty Salon and Sun Deck Bar from the forward Observation Deck, taken while the ship was still in the fitting out yard at Helsinki in 1984. The only real difference between this image and a modern one from the same place is the later addition of two satellite domes fitted behind the mast. (*Bernard Warner*)

or one large double bed by pushing them together. In the standard staterooms, one of the beds folded up during the day to provide more floor space. In addition to having ten wheel-chair accessible cabins, there were some adapted bathrooms on the accommodation decks. These could be used by anyone who could manage in a standard cabin, but needed extra help when bathing.

There were two acres of open deck, much of which was surfaced with traditional teak planking. This gave *Royal Princess* more deck space than any other cruise ship operating at the time. The Sun Deck also boasted one of the largest lap-pools afloat, holding 95 tons of water.

The Bridge was fitted with the latest communication and navigation systems. The satellite communication system was the Mascot 2000, designed and developed specifically for *Royal Princess*. This provided two-way data, voice, telex and fax transmissions. The main radio station incorporated new solid state transmitter/receiver equipment – the first of its kind to be used at sea – and there was a computer-guided automatic direction finder giving immediate longitude and latitude positions.

The most important technological advance was in the engine room. The main propulsion machinery consisted of four Wärtsilä Pielstick six-cylinder type PC4-2L engines, each capable of 9,900 horsepower and arranged in pairs. Designed in France and built at the Wärtsilä Engine Works at Turku, they gave *Royal Princess* a top speed of 22 knots, burning a single grade of high-viscosity fuel not previously on the market. This avoided the separate tanks required for carrying two different grades of fuel, which was the more usual arrangement, and gave the ship an unprecedented 80 per cent reduction in fuel costs compared with existing cruise ships operating at the time. The rear pair of engines were connected to a special gear box which allowed the power produced to drive a propeller and an alternator, either separately or both together. These alternators each generated sufficient power for the entire ship requirement of 6,600 volts. This was then transferred into the 440 and 220 volt current required for the ship's domestic services.

The twin rudders were each capable of independent control. This feature, together with two controllable-pitch, four-bladed propellers, each weighing 28 tons, and two bow thrusters, gave the ship excellent manoeuvrability. When Captain Bernard Warner (now Commodore Warner, master of the *Queen Mary 2*) took command briefly in 1996, this was the first time he had used independently controllable rudders on a ship and he remarked on how well the ship handled as a result. Indeed Captain Ian Tomkins, Relief Captain at

Above: The open deck area aft of the Lido Café with the Horizon Lounge above (still with protective film over the windows), pictured during further sea trials, 23 September 1984. (*Alan Mackenzie*)

Right: The Sun Deck lap pool with two circular splash pools either side, pictured on sea trials, 23 September 1984. The glass screens have white protective film over them and the Sun Deck Bar is still under construction. (*Alan Mackenzie*)

The wide teak Promenade Deck, starboard side looking forward. This picture is of *Artemis*, but there is little change here from her days as *Royal Princess*. The windows are those of passenger cabins and have one-way glass for privacy. The cylindrical containers on the right are emergency life rafts which open on contact with seawater. (*Andrew Sassoli-Walker*)

the time of her launch, commented, 'She's handling so much better even than expected … The only analogy I can see is like dancing with a beautiful lady in a crinoline dress when a Viennese waltz is playing.' Two fin stabilizers reduced roll in rough sea conditions.

Two water distillers produced together the 600 tonnes of fresh water needed every day by the 1,750 passengers and crew. Around 80 tonnes of this was used in the laundry alone, where a crew of ten washed 80,000 pieces of cabin linen, 30,000 tablecloths and napkins from the dining rooms and 14,000 deck towels every week. The heat required for the distillers was recycled from the main engine's cooling system. In fact, in a period not normally recognised as being particularly ecologically aware, *Royal Princess* was remarkable, not just for the efficient use of the engines in this way, but in the refuse disposal systems and the double glazed and tinted windows, which reduced demand on the air conditioning or heating, depending on itinerary.

Even the Galley concept was innovative. Since *Royal Princess* was almost

Above: The Bridge chart table, pictured while the ship was on sea trials, 21 September 1984. (*Alan Mackenzie*)

Right: Framed cut-away drawing of one of the four Pielstick engines, designed in France especially for *Royal Princess* and manufactured in Finland. This is mounted on the wall in the Engineering Department. (*Andrew Sassoli-Walker*)

Left: The twin propellers and rudders, photographed during dry docking in Bremerhaven, April 2010. Each four-bladed propeller is 5.2 metres (17 feet) in diameter and weighs 28 tons. This design of the propellers mounted immediately behind both rudders, and so forcing water over them, together with the option of independent rudder control, gives the ship excellent manoeuvrability. (*The Ship's Photographer*)

Below left: The twin port-side bow thrusters, pictured while the ship was in dry dock at Bremerhaven, 13 April 2010. These two transverse controllable-pitch thrusters, with stainless steel blades, are each 2 metres (6½ feet) in diameter and weigh 1.2 tons.

Below right: One of the two Sperry forward-folding, gyro-controlled fin stabilisers, seen here while *Artemis* was in dry dock in Bremerhaven, 13 April 2010. When deployed in rough seas, they will reduce the rolling of the ship by around 80 per cent with the ship travelling at a speed of 18 knots. When fully extended, they each measure 5.5 metres (18 feet).

double the size of the luxury cruise ships of the previous decades, she presented a challenge in ensuring the attention to detail in food preparation and service that Princess Cruises had become known for. In addition, stringent new international health and safety regulations had to be met. Clever design provided around 1,982 cubic metres (70,000 cubic feet) of food storage space, close to the galley and food preparation areas and linked with the refuse disposal systems. All stores arrived at the dockside on pallets and were loaded via a special lift. Once on board, the ship's forklift trucks took them to the correct store – frozen, chilled or dry – all located on Zero and One Decks. Special insulated carts would then be used to take food from these stores to the main, Lido or crew galleys as and when required. This system worked so well that it is still in use today. The catering staff were selected for *Royal Princess* a year before she was due to enter service so that they could be fully trained both in Princess Cruises standards and style as well as on the new equipment and systems.

The refuse disposal room contained two incinerators as well as a whole battery of special grinders and compressors to dispose of bottles, tins and other rubbish. Food waste went into a special pulper to extract any moisture. The water was then treated and put through a number of processes until it was changed into 'grey' water which was then disposed of when the ship was 19 kilometres (12 miles) or more away from any land. The remaining food

Above left: Sorting crew uniform shirts and cabin linen in the ship's laundry, March 2009. Every week, 80,000 pieces of cabin linen, 30,000 tablecloths and napkins and 14,000 deck towels were washed by the crew of ten.

Above right: John McMullan, Executive Chef on board *Artemis*, pictured in the galley, 1 August 2010. (*Andrew Sassoli-Walker*)

Two of *Artemis'* galley crew, with some very tempting desserts! The attention to detail even runs to the P&O Cruises rising sun logo piped onto the chocolate puddings. 1 August 2010. (*Andrew Sassoli-Walker*)

debris was burned or compressed into convenient sized blocks which were stored in a refrigerated room to eliminate any potential health hazards and then eventually disposed of at designated ports. Paper, wood and disposable items were burnt and the ashes landed ashore; cans were compressed and recycled ashore with other metals, and glass was crushed and similarly disposed of.

The best materials and most technologically advanced equipment for *Royal Princess* were sourced from all over the world. For example, the main engines were designed in France and made in Finland, but with gears from Holland and clutches from the UK. The air conditioning units were from Sweden, the water distillation plant, radar system, lifeboats and incinerators from the UK, the telephone system from France, the windows from Spain, the galley dishwashers and ice-making equipment from the USA, and the stabilisers from Japan. Of the £150 million contract, just £5 million was spent in Britain, whose companies also supplied many interior fittings such as blinds, deck furniture and cushions, 4,000 blankets, logo-printed paper napkins, cocktail sticks, galley and gymnasium scales, cabin coat hangers and restaurant silverware. The largest interior contract went to the Yorkshire firm of Tankard Carpets who fitted out all the public areas and some of the higher grade staterooms.

The first master of the ship was Captain John Young. Captain Young was born in Bristol on 1 October 1932. He began his career with P&O as a cadet officer in 1950, and after serving on both cargo and passenger ships, gained his master's certificate in 1959. His first appointment to senior command was in 1970 on the *Uganda*, a P&O educational cruise ship. From February 1975 he was Master of the *Sun Princess*, aside from one year in Australia as Captain of the *Oriana*. At the time he was appointed to *Royal Princess*, he was living in Weston-super-Mare, Somerset, with his wife, Jill, and daughter, Caroline. Another crew member from Weston-super-Mare was Deputy Purser Paul Brougham, whose field of expertise was in managing the new and complicated computer systems installed on *Royal Princess*.

Captain John Young at the forward console controls on the Bridge of *Royal Princess*, on her first arrival at Southampton, November 1984. (Southern Daily Echo)

The first of a series of sea trials took place in June 1984 with the final owner's acceptance trials three months later. At this time, every piece of equipment was tried and tested and any adjustments made. Before *Royal Princess* left the yard for her first voyage, journalists were shown over the ship by Captain Young, accompanied by her television 'master' Gavin MacLeod – Captain Stubing in *The Love Boat* series and advertising spokesman for Princess Cruises.

During the second half of 1984, Captain Young began making the final preparations before taking over as Master. Following a seven-week promotions tour in the USA and Canada, he, together with his Deputy Captain David Brown and Relief Captain Ian Tomkins, travelled to Copenhagen, Denmark, for further practice in controlling the ship using a simulator. 'It's a way of having your collisions in comfort,' he wryly commented at the time! Then induction training had to be undertaken for the 500-strong ship's company. Since *Royal Princess* had so much new technology on board, a great deal of familiarisation had to take place prior to entry into service. Much of this

Above: The original machinery operating manual is still in daily use today. (*Andrew Sassoli-Walker*)

Left: View of the bow of *Royal Princess* in the fitting-out berth in Helsinki, 27 October 1984. She was undergoing final finishing touches following sea trials and would shortly be ready for delivery to P&O. (*Alan Mackenzie*)

Open day in Helsinki, 27 October 1984, when local people were invited to look over *Royal Princess* before she sailed for Southampton. In the foreground is another new build, Hull 466, *Sea Goddess 1*. This ship, together with her sister *Sea Goddess 2*, were the first of a planned fleet of eight luxury cruise yachts. When the owners fell into financial difficulties, the ships were acquired by Cunard. When Cunard merged with Seabourn, this ship became *Seabourn Goddess 1*. She is still sailing today as *Seadream 1*. (*Alan Mackenzie*)

instruction took place in the famous Warsash Nautical College near P&O's home port of Southampton. In fact, a new shipboard department was created, which took into account the highly technological nature of the ship. This was appropriately named the Electro-Technical Department and was another of the many *Royal Princess* 'firsts'; it is now standard on every cruise ship. From the first cutting of the steel in Helsinki, P&O Technical Officers had been sent to the shipyard to work alongside the shipbuilders to learn about all the equipment and the maintenance required. As it turned out, the systems were so advanced that the ship's engineers often struggled to maintain them, and in her early years of service, Bernard Warner, then Chief Officer, recalls that the vessel was frequently prone to sudden blackouts and loss of power.

Up to the minute computer technology was also used for the running of the ship, including passenger billing, stock inventory and crew data. Keeping track of stock was crucial to the smooth running of a cruise. Passengers are not happy when the bar runs out of their favourite tipple! This equipment enabled the ship to be one of the first, if not the first, to offer a cashless system on board by passengers registering a credit card which was automatically debited at the end of a cruise. The use of computers even extended to the Engine Room, where they monitored the efficiency of the engines. Another *Royal Princess* 'first' was to have a dedicated Computer Officer solely responsible for these on-board systems.

Royal Princess was handed over to P&O on 30 October, one day ahead of the contract deadline. The following day she set sail on her positioning voyage to Southampton, running into sixty hours of thick fog and a force eight gale. Captain Young later commented on how well the ship handled and how good a test it had been for the new systems. Perhaps it was also a useful introduction to the characteristics of the ship with what was to become a rather 'interesting' crossing of the Atlantic on her maiden voyage! She arrived in Southampton on 5 November. That allowed ten days to apply the final finishing touches and make preparations for her naming ceremony on 15 November 1984.

CHAPTER 3

A ROYAL PRINCESS –
NAMING CEREMONY AND MAIDEN VOYAGE

Royal Princess arrived for the first time in Southampton on 5 November 1984. Paul Brougham remembers the occasion well! 'We were arriving at Southampton from Helsinki for our first call and I needed to go up to the Bridge to see how long we had before the officials boarded. The atmosphere on the Bridge can often be a little tense on these occasions and particularly so when it is a maiden call, highly publicised, plenty of press and media, including helicopters circling. This time I sensed there was more of an atmosphere than normal; in fact the tension was palpable. I soon discovered the reason why. The Captain, John Young, was trying to bring the ship alongside but the engines were not responding to his instruction for reverse. We were visibly going forward, at speed, heading towards the stern of the Martini ship that was tied up alongside in front. There were many expletives coming from the Captain and instructions being issued to use a manual override. I dared not move and was transfixed with the vision of the newest addition to the fleet, the much hailed and vaunted *Royal Princess* arriving in port for the first time since she sailed from Wärtsilä's shipyard, rear-ending the ship in front. All of this would be captured handsomely by the attending media! Fortunately we pulled back from the brink and got alongside. To this day whenever I see a bottle of Martini it reminds me of this near disaster, and inevitably I hum the tune from the television advert that was being shown at this time: "Martini, it's the right one, its Martini."' The then Chief Officer Bernard Warner added to this account that the day was actually saved by a tug that was made fast to the stern. On instructions from the Captain, she pulled the ship away from the dock and averted a collision with the tanker. 'Many mooring lines were already on the dock at that time and I recall them being paid out as quickly as

possible with a lot of tension on each one. The fear was that one might part and cause injury to the dignitaries waiting on the dock!'

During her brief stay at Southampton, *Royal Princess* was joined by the legendary SS *Canberra* who was at the time still basking in the glory of her sterling service in the Falklands Conflict two years earlier. The progress in ship design was clearly evident when the two ships were seen together. The one, traditional and solid, with inboard lifeboats, a straight stem and a noticeable sheer to the hull (the upward curve of the longitudinal lines of a ship's hull as viewed from the side); the other, sleek and streamlined with straight lines and pointed stem.

Thursday, 15 November 1984: *I Feel For You* by Chaka Khan was number one in the charts, the national Miners' Strike entered its eighth month, Ronald Reagan had just been elected President of the USA, and Diana, Princess of Wales, prepared to name the *Royal Princess* in Southampton. When the name was first chosen, it was discovered there was already a ship named *Royal Princess* registered in London. At P&O's request, however, the owners of the Thames pleasure steamer kindly agreed to change the port of registry of their boat to Gravesend, enabling the cruise liner to be registered at Lloyds of London.

It was not only HRH The Princess of Wales' first experience of ship-naming, but her first solo engagement without the support of Prince Charles by her side, and she was understandably somewhat nervous. P&O were also not going to take any chances that the magnum of vintage Krug champagne might not break against the bow (an ancient nautical superstition believed that occurrence would bring bad luck to the ship). The Chief Engineer, Charlie

Royal Princess berthed behind *Canberra* on her first arrival in Southampton, November 1984. Although similar in terms of gross tonnage, these two ships are worlds apart in design. Built in 1961, note the curve (sheer or sway) in the hull of *Canberra* (right) and the rounded stern. If you stood on a lower deck corridor and looked the length of the ship you would not be able to see the far end. *Canberra* was built using traditional methods of welding a frame together and then adding the hull plating. *Royal Princess* (left) is all sleek straight lines. This is due to the construction methods of welding prefabricated sections of hull together. Nevertheless, in her day, *Canberra* was hailed as 'ship of the century' when launched from the Belfast yard of Harland & Wolff. Her innovative design had the engines set aft instead of centrally to give more deck space and greater flexibility in the arrangement of her public rooms. (Southern Daily Echo)

Newby, had installed a large hinged metal cradle let loose by a heavy rope and had made numerous practice runs using cheap sparkling wine, especially as it was rumoured that his job was on the line if the bottle did not break first time! As the Princess emerged onto the quayside from her special train from London, 2,000 invited guests were there to greet her. She mounted the podium and waited while the Bishop of Southampton, the Rt Revd Edward Cartwright, blessed the vessel, before she uttered the classic words, 'I name this ship the *Royal Princess*. May God bless her and all who sail in her.' She then pulled the silver lever and the bottle splintered against the sparkling white bow.

Princess Diana was then escorted on a tour of the ship by the Senior Deck Cadet Ian Hutley (now captain of P&O Cruises' *Oriana*) as she met Captain John Young and the ship's company. Bernard Warner was then Chief Officer of *Royal Princess*. He particularly noted that she took the time to shake hands and speak to each and every crew member.

Left: HRH The Princess of Wales arrives at Southampton on 15 November 1984 to name *Royal Princess*. (Southern Daily Echo)

Below left: HRH The Princess of Wales pulls the lever to release the magnum of champagne against *Royal Princess'* hull. (Southern Daily Echo)

Below right: HRH The Princess of Wales being shown around the ship, accompanied by Captain Young and Lord Sterling (on her right), chairman of P&O. The party is standing outside the Horizon Lounge looking down onto the Lido Deck and Pool. (Southern Daily Echo)

Jenny Prince also recalls the preparations and naming day well. 'I had been at sea with P&O for nearly four years when I was seconded to work in the P&O Southampton office, preparing invitations to the naming ceremony. However, I was delighted to be taken off that role when I was summoned to join *Royal Princess* as an Assistant Purser (the only female officer in the team at that time) while she was still being built in the Wärtsilä shipyard in Helsinki. We initially stayed in the Helke Hotel, not somewhere I would rush back to and which suddenly made the invitations job seem not so bad, before more crew arrived and P&O chartered a ferry for us to live on in the latter building stages. We sailed out of Helsinki to Southampton, with what I presume was Sibelius' music broadcast over the tannoy, on the gloomiest, wet and miserable November day.

'I remember everyone getting quite nervous about the arrangements from the Palace for Princess Diana's arrival, as it was her first solo engagement, and there were endless planning meetings at which I had to take the minutes. Tim, a fellow Assistant Purser, and myself were put in charge of the press on the big day, which involved herding them together and making sure they didn't bump into Princess Diana and Captain Young as we all toured the ship. I'm not sure what happened but one of us went the wrong way and we were all tripping over sun-beds trying to keep out of the Royal party's way! I also recall being told that we could take the press downstairs once the President of Finland had passed, but none of us knew what he looked like! We were supposed to keep

Above left: HRH The Princess of Wales chatting to the master of *Royal Princess*, Captain John Young, at the naming ceremony, 15 November 1984. (*Stephen Radford*)

Above right: Captain John Young escorting HRH The Princess of Wales on a tour of the ship, 15 November 1984. The Pakistani crew are wearing their Pathan dress uniforms. (*Alan Mackenzie*)

them ensconced in a room, with a buffet, etc., laid on, but of course they all wanted to go away to file their story for the lunch time news so we rather gave up on trying to keep them hostage.'

James Cusick (currently Executive Purser on board P&O Cruises' *Oceana*) was another who was involved with the preparations for the launch. 'My fond memories (of the ship) are of the naming ceremony. Earlier that year when I was working on board *Sea Princess* (later *Victoria*) as a Junior Assistant Purser in the Crew Office, I arranged for a group of fifty crew members to visit the *Royal Princess* in Helsinki where the ship was being built. It was the first time I had been in a shipyard visiting a new build. This in itself was very exciting. However there was a lot more to come … I was on leave when asked to work on board the *Royal Princess* as a "tour guide"! My job was to show travel agents and other VIPs around the ship and then offer them a Champagne Afternoon Tea! I felt very privileged to be working on such a beautiful ship and the largest new ship in the P&O Princess Cruises Fleet! I even appeared on the "This Morning" TV show! I remember thinking how luxurious the suites were and dreamt that one day I would sail in the Princess Suite – it never did happen but we have to dream!

'The evening before the naming ceremony we had a rehearsal dinner on board. Everything was sparkling with the new silverware and fine china in use for the first time. On the naming day I remember Captain Young waiting at the top of the gangway to receive the Royal party. I was so excited to get a glimpse of Princess Diana – she was so beautiful and did a fantastic job at the naming, making everyone feel so at ease. All the finely tuned arrangements went with military precision on the day! I stayed on board in Stateroom D111. All the cabins were outboard – another first at that time for the cruising industry. With all the inaugural functions complete I disembarked and continued with my leave.'

The Princess left the ceremony laden down with gifts from the crew, owners and ship builders, including two P&O teddy bears for her sons, a set of Finnish gold jewellery from Wärtsilä, and a silver replica of the Spindrift sculpture that adorns the main atrium.

Some controversy was caused the day after the naming when the press reported that President Mauno Koivisto of Finland felt upstaged by the Princess during his official visit to Britain. *The Times* reported that at the naming ceremony he had to tag along in her wake while she chatted to crowds. 'I began to be increasingly convinced I was in a wrong place at a wrong time,' he is reported as saying. The entry for the President in The National Biography of Finland puts it, 'His wrath was perhaps more on behalf of the institution of the presidency than of himself as a person. The public were interested only in Princess Diana, who had been invited to the occasion, and the Finns did not

even get into the same stand with her. Koivisto's irritation was increased by the fact that some Princess-infatuated Finns curtseyed to her as if they were at court.'

Following her official naming ceremony, there was a two-day shake-down cruise to Guernsey before *Royal Princess* set sail on her maiden voyage – an eight-day transatlantic crossing to Florida. It was then planned to have three days of festivities in Miami before she sailed on her inaugural North American Cruise to her new home port of Los Angeles. Such had been the anticipation that the maiden voyage had sold out in just three hours, with fares ranging from £871 per person in a twin cabin to £2,111 for the top luxury suites. There was even a waiting list for cabins.

Ian Scott and his wife were on the maiden voyage leaving Southampton on 19 November 1984 – not the best time of year to be crossing the Atlantic in any ship (except perhaps one of the true transatlantic liners such as the now retired *Queen Elizabeth 2*, which was designed for exactly that task)! They were in a Promenade Deck cabin. As the ship approached the Bay of Biscay the weather deteriorated rapidly, and the decks were closed as the waves began to crash over the bow. Ian then recalled the weather became so severe that glass doors were wrenched from their hinges and wine glasses, crockery and cutlery were lying all over the floor of the main dining room. One of the satellite communication domes ended up in the Sun Deck lap pool. P&O Princess executives, occupying the top-grade suites on the upper decks, were literally thrown from their beds as cabin televisions crashed around them. As James Cusick later commented, 'The passengers and ship's company on the maiden voyage had one they would never forget, experiencing some rough weather and enjoying some unplanned days at sea! It was then we found out that the cabin televisions needed to be screwed down!'

Bernard Warner also recalls that voyage well. Low pressure areas around Biscay and the Canaries caused the worst seas he had ever seen in all his time at sea, before or since. For two to three days the ship struggled through 30 to 40 foot waves. Every time she rose out of a trough and then began to pitch heavily, the bow occasionally pounded down with a deafening noise. P&O's project manager, David McKee, was on board for the crossing and spent a lot of time on the Bridge. He even considered changing the design of her bow to try and reduce the noise in case any similar weather conditions were experienced in the future. At the time, Captain Young cut the speed of the ship to reduce the pounding, and even hove to for several hours, meaning that he brought the ship round to face into the prevailing sea and made very slow speed until the storm passed over.

Paul Brougham, then Deputy Purser, remembered, 'The maiden voyage of a ship attracts a certain type of passenger; perhaps they like the kudos of

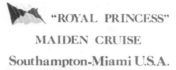

Left: Front cover of the *Southern Evening Echo* special supplement, published to mark the maiden voyage of *Royal Princess*. (Southern Evening Echo)

Above: Special commemorative franked envelopes to mark the naming ceremony and maiden voyage of *Royal Princess*, November 1984. (*Author's Collection*)

The Royal Marines Band play on the Southampton quayside amid streamers as *Royal Princess* departs on her maiden voyage to Miami, 19 November 1984. It was to be some ten years before she returned to Southampton. (Southern Daily Echo)

informally. Crossing the stormy Atlantic was not going to interrupt this event and so those able to attend made their way to the wardroom, which was located high up, just below the Bridge at the forward end of the ship. The weather was very rough, access to the outside decks was prohibited to passengers, and sick bags were available throughout the ship (for passengers and crew). Many of the crew were unwell, but the passengers, in the main, were well travelled and experienced and they lapped up the extreme conditions. On arrival in the wardroom the food was being kept hot in chafing dishes on a buffet table (which was secured to a hand rail), all the officers were strung out around the perimeter of the room, legs apart for balance and hanging on to the handrail and in their other hand they held a drink and/or cigarette. Conversation was muted by the thunder of the waves as the ship ploughed in to trough after trough and she shuddered forward. Some waves were crashing up and the spray splashing against the wardroom windows. There is a 'Kodak' moment with the room shaking, the air hot and humid filled with the smell of food and cigarettes, the windows being splashed and the overwhelming sense that the officers were only there in order to say that they made it!'

Jenny Prince continues the story, 'We departed in November ... and it was the first time I had sailed with British passengers, who were not the easiest I had come across. Mind you, there was a lot to moan about, albeit out of P&O's hands, and that was the weather – it was horrifically rough. It was difficult to sleep with all the crashing and banging going on and I was glad I was going on leave in Miami, although my relief, Nicky, took one look at how tired we all looked and nearly turned round and walked back down the gangway. The second night of the cruise Peter, a fellow Assistant Purser, discovered an old gentleman in his pyjamas loitering in the atrium area near the closed Purser's office. Peter thought he'd finish his rounds and then escort him back to his cabin. However, by the time he returned there was an atrium full of people, many of whom had actually donned their life jackets, all trying to get some respite from the rocking by being in the centre of the ship, so it was tea and sandwiches all round! I remember I spent an inordinate amount of time typing telexes from passengers informing all and sundry back in the UK that they would be late back.'

Royal Princess eventually arrived in Miami two days late, leaving pre-arranged hotel stays and excursion plans in tatters. Not the greatest start to a ship's career, and consequently there was very little time to repair the not-inconsiderable damage caused during the crossing before setting sail again on a seventeen-day voyage to the Caribbean, then through the Panama Canal (where it was planned to film a special episode of *The Love Boat* on board) to Los Angeles.

being the first to travel. However, they also have to put up with any teething problems that can arise. The *Royal Princess* had many innovations but in the end she was essentially a ship afloat on the high seas and travelling across the Atlantic in late November has its own risks. We encountered bad weather and as a result were going to be late arriving in Fort Lauderdale. Nonetheless, the officers had the tradition of having a 'pub lunch' in the wardroom every Sunday. The event provided a way to socialise together and talk over issues

CHAPTER 4

THE PRINCESS YEARS 1984-2005

With the demand for luxury cruising from the West Coast of the USA and the Caribbean in a continual upward trend, the intention was for *Royal Princess* to be operated by the US arm of Princess Cruises. This was the reason that a West Coast American company had been involved in the interior design and décor. At the same time that the new flagship was launched, the other ships in the fleet – *Sun*, *Island* and *Pacific Princesses* all had extensive interior renovations to bring them closer to the standard of *Royal Princess*.

In 1984, three inaugural cruises were advertised, the first of which was a seventeen-night Panama Canal Cruise from Miami to Los Angeles, leaving on 29 November and calling at St Thomas, Antigua, Barbados, Cartagena, Panama City, Acapulco and Cabo San Lucas.

From the start this was going to be the media event of the year. A special two-hour episode of *The Love Boat* was being filmed on board, with guest stars Lana Turner, Anne Baxter and Stewart Granger. While on board, Stewart Granger is remembered for ordering a large pitcher of Bloody Marys from the Lido Bar every day at noon and then walking around refilling passengers' glasses while they relaxed on the deck on sun loungers! Passengers also vied with each other to appear as extras on the show and the crew were bemused that there were more people indoors watching the filming than outside watching the transit of the Panama Canal. Also on board for part of the cruise were a television crew from A.M. Chicago, with the then unknown presenter Oprah Winfrey. This local morning programme later became the *Oprah Winfrey Show*.

When *Royal Princess* finally arrived in Los Angeles, she was welcomed to her new home with a big reception on board. Among the guests were Joan Collins, Vincent Price, Caesar Romero, and the executive producer of *The Love Boat*, Aaron Spelling with his wife.

The next two voyages were a ten-night Christmas Cruise to the Mexican Riviera calling at Puerto Vallarta, Manzanillo, Acapulco, then Christmas Day at sea, Mazatlan, Cabo San Lucas and back to Los Angeles, followed by a fourteen-night New Year's cruise through the Panama Canal again to the Caribbean, finishing in San Juan.

From then on the ship's first few years were spent in the Caribbean in winter and Alaska in the summer. After twelve more cruises through the Panama Canal with three varying itineraries of ten, eleven or fourteen nights, *Royal Princess* was repositioned to San Francisco for the first of thirteen ten-night round-trip cruises to Alaska. These were also based on a standard itinerary visiting Vancouver, Juneau, cruising Glacier Bay, Sitka, Victoria, and back to San Francisco. As summer drew to a close, *Royal Princess* headed south to recommence the Panama Canal and Mexican Riviera cruises.

Life on board for the passengers revolved around the usual cruising occupations of eating, deck games (table-tennis, shuffleboard, deck quoits and trap-shooting from the stern), eating, exploring ashore, eating, sunbathing, eating, evening entertainment, and more eating!

The Continental Dining Room on Deck Two (Plaza Deck) seated 616 and was on two levels across the full width of the ship. This allowed diners spectacular sea views through the large windows at each side of the dining room. The carpets and curtains were in shades of beige and turquoise with silver threads. This contrasted with the chairs of chromium-plated tubular steel upholstered in red or turquoise. The first Head Chef was Italian Alfredo

Clockwise from top: Illuminated charter celebrating the arrival of *Royal Princess* – 'the World's Most Exciting Resort' – at her new home port of Los Angeles, 16 December 1984. This still hangs on the Bridge of *Artemis*. (*Andrew Sassoli-Walker*)

Captain John Young (centre) with Deputy Captain David Brown (left) and Chief Officer Bernard Warner (right) on the port bridge wing as *Royal Princess* berths in Ketchikan, Alaska, October 1985. (*Bernard Warner*)

Brenda Crombie-Noble (left) and Diane Jones photographed on their way ashore at Cozumel, Mexico, 4 May 2002. They found a secret sunbathing spot on board (p.57). (*Diane Jones*)

The images on this page illustrate all the major landmarks on the Panama Canal. Opening on 15 August 1914, the canal was a major engineering achievement and cut days off a ship's journey to the Pacific Ocean, not to mention the potential risks to shipping in having to round the notorious Cape Horn. The average transit time of the Canal is nine hours, passing through three sets of locks which raise ships the 85 feet up from sea level required to pass through the Gaillard Cut through the Continental Divide and then back down again to sea level. Artificial lakes created by dammed rivers supply the water required for the locks. Throughout the journey passengers can enjoy the stunning scenery which surrounds the Canal including the Parque Nacional Isla Barro Colorado in the middle of Lake Gatun.

Above left: Commodore Mike Moulin and the local pilot on board *Royal Princess* in the Gatun Locks at the Caribbean entrance to the Panama Canal, May 2002. Note the canvas bridge wing awning. This was used for transits of the Panama Canal when the Bridge officers spent a lot of time out on the wing. (*Diane Jones*)

Above right: *Artemis* in the Gatun Locks, Panama Canal, 31 December 2007. Note the two locomotives (called mules) either side of the ship. Four of these pull every ship through the locks, keeping them centred in the narrow canal basins. (*The Ship's Photographer*)

Right: *Artemis* in the Gatun Locks, Panama Canal, 15 January 2009. She is in the topmost of the three basins and about to exit into the Gatun Lake. (*The Ship's Photographer*)

Left: Artemis in the Gatun Locks at the Atlantic entrance to the Panama Canal, 15 January 2009. (*The Ship's Photographer*)

Below left: Royal Princess passing *Sea Princess* in the Gatun Lake in the Panama Canal, 26 January 1985. The picture was taken from the top of the funnel. Unusually, both ships are dressed overall, despite being 'at sea'. Was this in honour of the meeting of the two sisters I wonder? (*Alan Mackenzie*)

Below right: Artemis in the Gaillard Cut in the Panama Canal, 15 January 2009. This is the narrowest part of the Canal, only wide enough for one ship at any one time. (*The Ship's Photographer*)

Right: Artemis sailing under the New Millennium Bridge, 7 December 2008. This is between Gamboa and the Pedro Miguel Locks which can be seen in the distance. (*The Ship's Photographer*)

Below left: Artemis in the Pedro Miguel Locks on the Panama Canal, 12 February 2010. (*The Ship's Photographer*)

Below right: Artemis entering the Miraflores Locks at the Pacific end of the Panama Canal. (*The Ship's Photographer*)

Above left: Artemis preparing to enter the Miraflores Locks, 7 December 2008. In the background are Panama City and the Bridge of the Americas leading to the Pacific Ocean. (*The Ship's Photographer*)

Above right: Traditional deck games such as shuffleboard and deck quoits (seen here) are still as popular today as they have ever been. May 2010. (*Sharon Poole*)

Marzi. At the age of just thirty-six, he was responsible for producing menus to appeal to the mainly American clientele, with delicacies such as lobster, crab, prime ribs and caviar featuring strongly on the seven-course dinner menus and five-course lunch menus. In charge of the dining room was the Maître d'hôtel Renzo Rotti, who was from Piedmont, the same region of Italy as the Chef. Head-waiters would prepare some of the food, such as Cherry Jubilee, in a table-side spectacular, enjoyed even by those around who had not chosen that particular dish. The Lido Café on Deck Eight (Lido Deck) offered a selection of salads, pasta and deserts, with different selections daily. At night it was transformed into a bistro and pizzeria. Every day the sixty galley staff prepared 3,600 main meals for passengers, as well as afternoon tea, the midnight buffet and light snacks in the Lido Café. For their part, passengers daily ate their way through one ton of meat and poultry, a quarter of a ton of fish, three quarters of a ton of vegetables, a quarter of a ton of flour, 3,000 eggs, 2,000 pieces of fresh fruit, 4,000 baked rolls and 1,500 pastries, the latter two items baked fresh each day. In the eight passenger bars and two crew bars, the average weekly consumption included 1,400 bottles of wine, 200 bottles of champagne and 500 bottles of spirits. Seven tons of ice was produced on board each day.

On boarding, the first part of the ship passengers would normally see was the atrium, called The Plaza. This was centrally positioned on Deck Two or Plaza Deck, and was the location for the Reception Desk, Tour Desk and entrance to the Continental Dining Room. It was dominated by a large steel sculpture of herring gulls with a fountain at its base. Entitled 'Spindrift', it was designed by David Norris, Fellow and one-time vice-president of the Royal Society of British Sculptors. Born in Brazil, David Norris studied sculpture at the Royal Academy School, London, winning the Portraiture Medal and the Landseer prize for composition. He produces both figurative and abstract pieces, large and small, in bronze, stainless steel and precious metals with birds featuring strongly in his work.

Paul Brougham, then Deputy Purser, recounts a couple of stories relating to this fountain: 'On Plaza Deck in the centre of the floor there was a sculpture of seagulls in flight called "Spindrift". The sculpture was stood in a fountain which was, I believe, the first fountain at sea on a P&O ship. It was controlled by equipment in the purser's office. This allowed one to manage the height of the water and avoid splashing the carpet. The pump could be turned off to allow cleaning, etc. The purser was Alan Hale, a well respected man with great experience. However, he seemed to have a thing about the fountain and he was often referred to as the "Chief Fountaineer". Once again humour got involved. The first time was the addition of a couple of gnomes, just before the Captain's cocktail party. One gnome even had a fishing rod and was placed on the side of the fountain. They were only noticed half-way through the party after which an investigation ensued as to who was responsible but the culprit was never found. I believe that Captain Young found the event amusing.

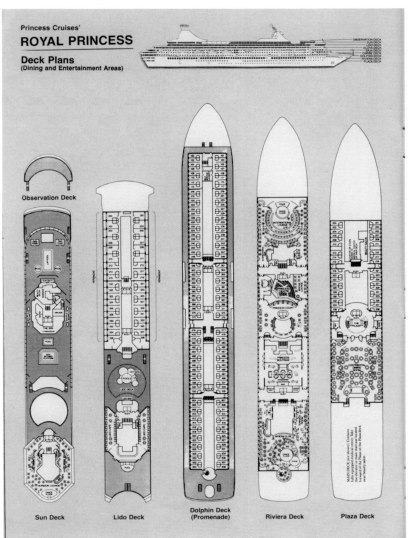

Left: The Continental Dining Room, April 1989. It seems there was no choice of bread roll, since they are already placed on the side plates! (*Paul Newland*)

Above: Deck plans of the public areas, 1988. (*Princess Cruises*)

'The second incident involved soap! A person or persons unknown during the course of the night added some soap powder to the fountain and by the morning the fountain was flowing over with bubbles! Once again the Chief Fountaineer investigated but the prankster was never found although there was a good deal of speculation as to their identity!'

Forward on the same deck were thirty-eight standard twin cabins as well as the Hairdressing Salon, a satellite credit card telephone booth and lifts and stairs leading down to the Medical Centre on Deck One (Main Deck). Also situated on Deck Two, although unseen by passengers, were the main offices for the Purser's department (including Accommodation and Catering Pursers) and the Computer Officer. From The Plaza, two sweeping staircases led up either side of the lift tower to the Princess Court piano lounge on Deck Three (Riviera Deck). A portrait of the ship's godmother, Princess Diana, graced this room, as indeed (at the time of writing) it still does.

Riviera Deck was the location for most of the remaining public areas. At the forward end was the International Show Lounge and bar. This room was laid out like a small amphitheatre, with tiered seating arranged around a large, almost central stage, ensuring the maximum interaction between a performer and their audience. Evening shows could be a traditional production number, a magician, comedian or a classical pianist. As on any cruise ship, every public space has to be multi-functional so it can be used both during the day and at night. The International Lounge was also the venue for daytime lectures, daily bingo sessions and as a muster station for shore excursions. Two long promenades with large picture windows ran down each side of the ship from here. On the starboard side, passengers walked from the International Lounge, through the Bridge Lounge (with seating for sixty-six card players) into the Princess Court, and then past the Princess Boutique and Crown Casino and Bar (with six blackjack tables, one craps table, a roulette table and 102 slot machines), through the Terrace Room to the Riviera Club. By day, this large space was used as a lounge, or for dancing lessons. At night, it became a sophisticated nightclub with its dance floor and small circular stage. Walking back up the port side, passengers went through the Riviera Bar, past the shop and casino again (both of which ran nearly the full width of the ship), through the Princess Court and into the Library and Photo Gallery before arriving back at the International Lounge. In the centre of the ship, between the International Lounge and Princess Court, was the Princess Theatre, which was used as a cinema, showing up-to-the-minute movies, and a stage for small-scale presentations and lectures. The Theatre and The Plaza were the only public areas with no outside views.

The next four decks up, Dolphin (Deck Four), Caribe (Deck Five), Baja (Deck Six) and Aloha (Deck Seven) were accommodation decks, the latter having all balcony staterooms. Dolphin Deck was the boat deck and had a wrap

Spindrift, the stainless steel sculpture of herring gulls by David Norris, is at the heart of the ship in the Atrium. At its base is a small bubbling fountain. The photograph is of *Artemis*, but nothing is greatly different here from her days as *Royal Princess*, except there were more plants around then. The doors on the lower deck lead into the Coral Dining Room. (*Andrew Sassoli-Walker*)

Above left: The International Lounge, November 1989. On the back wall are some mixed media on gesso panels. These were produced by Anthony Benjamin from the UK, and were part of the specially commissioned artworks for the ship. (*John Blewitt*)

Above right: The Festival Theatre or Princess Theatre as it was called when the ship was *Royal Princess*. As well as showing films, this venue was used for daytime lectures such as maritime history or the popular talks on jewellery. (*Andrew Sassoli-Walker*)

around teak promenade on which three and a half laps equalled one mile. Each passenger deck had a small lounge area in the midships stair tower, with chairs and sofas, coffee tables, writing desks, and plants. A few years after the ship's launch, the library was moved to this area on Deck Four. On Aloha Deck, this space included a communal balcony on both port and starboard sides. On Lido Deck (Deck Eight) were the two penthouse suites, twelve suites and twenty-four deluxe staterooms. All the cabins were decorated in a manner to make passengers feel at home. For example, valances were added to the beds so they looked less like ships' bunks, and other textiles such as scatter cushions softened the decor. The cabin televisions were not just for entertainment, but also carried a full teletext ship-board information channel on which passengers were able to access wine lists, menus and daily activity programmes. The original idea had been to dispense with the Princess Patter printed programme and daily shipboard newspaper, but these were soon re-instated due to passenger demand (you cannot carry a television screen round the decks with you to see what is on where!).

Aft of the suites were the Lido Bar and pool area leading to the Lido Café. This was in two halves either side of the funnel; one allowed smoking, the other side was non-smoking. They were linked at the aft end by the food servery. Another credit card satellite telephone booth was positioned on the starboard side of the Lido Deck foyer. Aft again of the café was a deck terrace with tables, a small pool and water feature. Originally this featured colourful umbrellas over the tables until they started to disappear overboard in inclement weather! Forward of the staterooms on this deck were the Bridge, wardroom and some more offices. At least once during each cruise, an open day was held on the Bridge, so that anyone interested could visit and look around.

Up on Deck Nine (Sun Deck) midships were the Games Arcade, Spa and Gymnasium. The latter comprised a fully equipped health and beauty suite with exercise machines, two saunas, massage rooms and an indoor whirlpool bath. There were two shuffleboard courts on the deck either side of the Gym and two table-tennis tables forward of the lap pool in the shade under the observation deck (there were more deck game courts on the tiered stern decks). The Sun Deck Bar faced the lap pool, which was one of the largest at sea and was flanked by two circular splash pools. Forward of the glass screen sheltering the pool was another spacious observation deck. Aft of the Spa and Gym was a smaller paddling pool and sun bathing platform and at the stern, the Horizon Lounge. By day this was the perfect place to relax with its spectacular 360 degree view of the passing world. At night, with the use of special lighting and sound equipment, this became a disco.

Left: An unobstructed view twin cabin C115, with the fold-down bed on the right, May 1989. During the day this was folded up and three bolsters were placed at the back of the other bed to create a sofa. At night they could be used as two single beds or one pushed up against the fold-down bed and made-up as a double. Compare this photograph with the one of the same cabin on page 96 taken twenty-one years later! (*Paul Newland*)

Below left: The sign on the Promenade Deck for walkers and joggers. The arrows are to encourage everyone to walk in one direction – in our experience it never works! Behind the sign the ship's IMO number is painted on the beam. This is a unique number assigned by the International Maritime Organisation for identification purposes. It never changes during the lifetime of the ship even if the ship has multiple different names, uses and registries. Also listed is the Net Tonnage of the ship – 19,744 tons – and the current Official Number of *Artemis* – 705797. This is allocated by the Registry of Shipping and Seamen and unlike the IMO number, it does change if the ship changes names or is registered to a different port. *Artemis'* ON number changed when her registry was moved from London to Hamilton, Bermuda. (*Andrew Sassoli-Walker*)

Below right: The passenger lounge area in the midships stair tower on Caribe Deck, May 1989. There was one of these on each of the main accommodation decks, the one on Aloha Deck also having public balconies instead of windows. When the ship was transferred to P&O in 2005, the furniture and books in these lounges were moved as they did not meet the upgraded SOLAS (Safety of Life at Sea) regulations, having been assessed as a fire risk in a main stairwell. (*Paul Newland*)

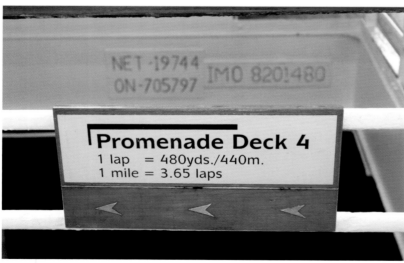

PRINCESS PATTER

M.V. ROYAL PRINCESS   MONDAY, AUGUST 31st, 1992   TILBURY, England
Tonight's Dress: CASUAL   ☾ Sunset: 7:44 pm

WELCOME ABOARD

The Captain, **JOHN KING**,
and the Officers and Crew
take pleasure in welcoming you aboard " Royal Princess "
On this cruise every effort will be made to make this a memorable experience.

Captain **John King** *was born in Newcastle - upon -Tyne, England. He started his schooling at Darjeeling in India and completed his education in Sheffield, England. He came to sea in 1953 and his first ship was a troop ship to Korea. Since then, he has served in a variety of ships including cargo ships to India, Africa, Australasia and the Far East, passenger ships worldwide, school ships in Scandinavia and the Mediterranean and a schooner around the British coast. He has a grown up family and lives at Newcastle in the North East of England.*

SENIOR OFFICERS

Deputy Captain	**BERNIE WARNER**	Purser	**CLIVE MILNE-BUCKLEY**
Chief Engineer Officer	**IAN BROWN**	Deputy Purser	**SONIA JOHNSON**
First Engineer Officer	**DAVID MITCHELL**	Chief Steward	**GIUSEPPE ARRIGO**
Chief Officer	**BOB OLIVER**	Chef de Cuisine	**ANTONIO CEREDA**
Chief Electro-Technical Officer	**TOM BECK**	Cruise Director	**JOHN LAWRENCE**
Doctor	**BOB EVANS**		

Above left: There were two of these publicly accessible balconies on the ship, on A Deck midships. In December 2007, they were incorporated into two new Superior Deluxe balcony staterooms, with four similar staterooms added in the same area on the two decks below. (*Carlos Price*)

Left: Alan Mackenzie, First Electronics Officer in the Broadcast Control Room, 17 May 1985. Besides offering several commercial channels of television, *Royal Princess* had its own broadcast teletext channel, which informed passengers of everything they needed to know about the ship – what was on, shore excursions, disembarkation procedures and even the wine list. (*Alan Mackenzie*)

Above right: Copy of the daily programme *Princess Patter*, for the first day of a cruise sailing from Tilbury, 31 August 1992. (*Andrew Sassoli-Walker*)

Left: The Lido pool and bar with fresh-water Jacuzzis and splash pools, 1990. On the Sun Deck is the Horizon Lounge. (*Princess Cruises*)

Above: Another view from the funnel top of *Royal Princess* while sailing through the Panama Canal, 26 January 1985. In the foreground is the Lido Pool. Forward of that is the Sun Deck with its sun bathing platform, the gymnasium, and furthest forward, the Observation Deck, crowded with people watching the transit. (*Alan Mackenzie*)

Left: The pool area on the forward sun deck, photographed while the ship was at Civitavecchia, the port of Rome, April 1989. The stairs on the left lead up to the observation deck. The sun loungers had matching striped terry towelling slipcovers over them; 'One of the many deluxe touches that make *Royal Princess* so special,' went the advertising blurb! (*Paul Newland*)

Above: The forward lap pool with the Princess Seawitch logo in tiles on the floor, May 1989. This was the largest at sea at the time, holding 95 tons of sea water. (*Paul Newland*)

Left: The Horizon Lounge of *Royal Princess*, 1984. Situated at the top of the ship at the stern, it offered virtually 360 degree views of the sea. In the day it was the perfect place to relax, read or chat to fellow passengers. In the late evening it became a nightclub. (*Brendan Coory*)

Above: One of a pair of ceramic wall features suggesting the wave motion of the sea and the forms and textures of the sea bed. It was designed and made by Barry Guppy of the UK and was part of the original artwork commissioned for *Royal Princess*. (*Andrew Sassoli-Walker*)

Below: One of the alcoves in the Starlight Lounge of *Artemis*. This was the Riviera Club under Princess. The textile wall hanging is made from tufted wool. It was designed by Rib Bloomfield from the UK, and manufactured at the John French Studio. The Lurex embellishment on it was woven by Jo Lang. This was another of the specially commissioned artworks for *Royal Princess* that still decorate the ship. Note, although *Artemis* is now exclusively for adults, there are still references to children's lifejackets being available (see sign on right)! (*Sharon Poole*)

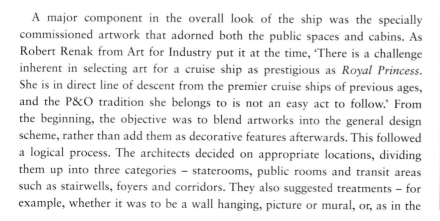

A major component in the overall look of the ship was the specially commissioned artwork that adorned both the public spaces and cabins. As Robert Renak from Art for Industry put it at the time, 'There is a challenge inherent in selecting art for a cruise ship as prestigious as *Royal Princess*. She is in direct line of descent from the premier cruise ships of previous ages, and the P&O tradition she belongs to is not an easy act to follow.' From the beginning, the objective was to blend artworks into the general design scheme, rather than add them as decorative features afterwards. This followed a logical process. The architects decided on appropriate locations, dividing them up into three categories – staterooms, public rooms and transit areas such as stairwells, foyers and corridors. They also suggested treatments – for example, whether it was to be a wall hanging, picture or mural, or, as in the

She may have been designed as a luxury ship for passengers, but little of the crew areas received the same treatment. This is the midships crew stairway and lift. (*Andrew Sassoli-Walker*)

case of the atrium, a sculpture. Then the interior designers chose the specific pieces, selecting work from a broad range of American and British artists. The common theme in all the art was that it was modern, in keeping with the contemporary style of the ship. In total, thirty artists, the majority of whom were young, were commissioned to produce a wide range of works including lithographs, watercolours, glass murals, collages, etchings, pastels, oil paintings, textiles, screen-prints and ceramic tiles.

Another important decorative element was greenery. Live tropical plants were used in most of the public areas. Weeping figs (ficus benjamina) were stationed in stairwells and altogether some 1,700 plants were arranged in 175 different containers, both inside and outside the ship. There were even plants around the Lido pool area.

There are those passengers who perhaps do not realise the numbers of crew on board or the complex organisation which goes towards the seamless running of a ship; some have even been reputed to ask, 'Do the crew sleep on board?' This may be an apocryphal question asked of one captain (to which the sardonic reply is said to have been, 'No, they are helicoptered off each night!'), but the answer on *Royal Princess* would have been yes, on the lower two decks. The majority of the ratings were accommodated in two berth cabins on Deck Zero, with higher ranking crew on Deck One, which was also the location for the mess rooms. Officers were accommodated on Deck Two in single cabins, with the senior officers allocated two-room suites.

As was usual with Princess ships at that time, the captain and senior officers were British, a maritime tradition that parent company P&O had maintained since the nineteenth century. In fact, despite the ship being US based, they were the largest national group on board, and included most cabin stewards and stewardesses. The Chef de Cuisine, Maître d'hôtel, catering and restaurant staff were Italian, and the remaining crew were drawn from all over the world.

The ship's officers were organised in the following groups:

Deck Officers

Captain
Deputy Captain
Chief Engineer
First Officer
Second Officer
Third Officer

Engineer's Department

Chief Engineer Officer
Second Engineer Officer
Junior Second Engineer Officer
Three Third Engineer Officers:
Third Engineer Officer (Maintenance)
Third Engineer Officer (Ventilation)
Assistant Engineer Officer

Electro-Technical Department (a department first introduced for *Royal Princess*)

Chief Electro-Technical Officer
First Electronic Officer
First Electrical Officer
Second Electronic Officer
Second Electrical Officer
Third Electronic Officer
Senior Assistant Electrical Officer
Assistant Electrical Officer

Purser's Department

Purser
Deputy Purser
Two Senior Assistant Pursers
Accommodation Officer
Three Assistant Pursers (Catering)
Three Assistant Pursers (Administration)

Medical Department

Surgeon
Assistant Surgeon
Two Nursing Officers

Entertainment

Cruise Director
Assistant Cruise Director
Plus about twenty-one guest entertainers and thirty-two concessionaires in the shops, spa, salon, etc.

A Day in the Life of a Deck Cadet

Robert W. Aldous, joined *Royal Princess* in 1986 at the age of seventeen, spending nine months on board as a Deck Cadet. The ship was then on a series of repeat Mexican Riviera itineraries of Acapulco to San Juan. Here he describes a typical day for him when the ship was in port.

0430hrs, Wake up call from the Officer of the Watch (OOW). Thirty minutes notice for collecting pilot at pilot station for ship's arrival at port.

0500hrs, At the pilot embarkation door, communications check with the Bridge. Await instruction. Rig – white boiler suit.

0515hrs, Open the starboard pilot door and rig the pilot embarkation ladder one metre above the waterline.

0530hrs, Embark pilot – deck cadet to escort pilot to the Bridge – prepare teas and coffees for all Officers.

0600hrs, Proceed to the forecastle and prepare mooring and heaving lines with the deck crew (Bosun, A.B.s, etc.).

0630hrs, Vessel enters the harbour breakwater. Deck cadet provides distances from the bow to any obstruction whilst Captain manoeuvres ship in a confined space.

0700hrs, Moor the *Royal Princess* with six head lines and two springs starboard side to.

0715hrs, Change of rig required to attend the Officers' Mess for breakfast: Rig – whites (tropical). American fry-up (very tough/crispy bacon, links sausages and powdered scrambled eggs).

0745hrs, Change of rig back into boiler suit for day work operations on deck. Meet the Chief Officer in his office, starboard side aft of Bridge.

0810hrs, Commence work on deck with the coxswains – typical work would include splicing wire into strops, splicing manila line into tricing pennants for lifeboats. Other duties would include greasing and oiling essential mooring gear and its associated equipment such as windlasses, Old Man leads, drum ends, etc.

0930hrs, Man Over-Board drill – exercise involving deck officers, engineers and medical staff. Aim: to launch the rescue boat within five minutes and recover a dummy from the water, return to ship and pass to medics for attention.

1000hrs, Full crew drill – exercise involving all crew. Fire scenario in a passenger cabin, deck cadet to wear fire suit and breathing apparatus, enter the cabin in a team of two, assume the fire is out of control, find a casualty and evacuate area. Assume fire desperately out of control and make all crew muster at life boats ready to abandon ship. Lower all outboard side lifeboats to embarkation level on Promenade Deck, embark several crew to each boat and lower to water to practice driving and searching for casualties.

1130hrs, Raise and secure all lifeboats.

1230hrs, Change back into whites – attend lunch in the Officers' Mess.

1330hrs, Remain in whites and relieve Coxswain at the gangway for his lunch break. (This was the security watch for the ship prior to global threats of terrorism).

1430hrs, Visit Second Officer on Bridge (Second Officer was Tim Stringer and was also cadet training officer). Show all coursework completed over the last week, oral test of some rules of the road, be quizzed on general seamanship, have completed tasks signed off in training book, be allocated new tasks to be completed by next week.

1500hrs, Change rig into boiler suit, meet with deck crew and be assigned work. Chip all paint from the aft mooring deck sets of 'bits'. Once chipped, re-paint.

1630hrs, Change of rig to whites to attend navigational briefing on Bridge. All deck officers present. Navigator informs crew of vessel movements, speeds, courses, etc., for the next three ports of call. Captain provides overview of cruise progress, expected functions for officers to attend. Deputy Captain discusses departmental issues.

1730hrs, Change of rig to boiler suit to attend the forecastle for letting go of the mooring lines upon departure.

1800hrs, All lines let go – collect pilot from the Bridge and escort him to the pilot door. Once away, aid the closure of the door and make secure for sea.

1830hrs, Change of rig to whites, attend the Bridge and relieve the helmsman of steering duties, orders to steer provided by the Captain or Officer of the Watch.

2000hrs, Change of rig to formal Mess Kit to attend Captain's Cocktail Party in Atrium and consume as much free champagne as possible!

2030hrs, Proceed to main restaurant. Passenger table entertained. Complimentary wine. My favourite meal was Beef Wellington followed by Baked Alaska .

2200hrs, Attend the Officers' Wardroom for a 'quiet beer' to relax after a long day! Unfortunately forbidden to attend crew disco in Crew Bar later due to only being a cadet.

Like most ships, there will be the occasional romance, but how many end up with a wedding? Bernard Warner (currently Master of the *Queen Mary 2* and Commodore of the Cunard fleet) met his future wife on board *Royal Princess* in 1986. He was Chief Officer at the time and on duty on the Bridge while the ship was in port. He saw a young lady walking along the dockside pulling a wheeled suitcase. He asked his colleague if he knew who she was and was told that she was the new beauty salon manageress, Tina Wimbush. Deciding his hair needed trimming he lost no time in making an appointment, only to be assigned someone else to do the cutting. Undeterred he went back soon afterwards for his beard to be trimmed. The rest, as they say, is history and they have been happily married ever since.

Diane Jones tells the story of when she was on board in May 2002 with her mother Brenda, and friend Brenda Crombie-Noble. At that time the stairs up from the promenade deck to the forward observation decks were closed to passengers, so the only access was via the accommodation passages on B and C decks. This meant climbing up a very high step to get out onto the deck, but it also meant that not many passengers ever found these decks. Both avid sunbathers, Diane and Brenda took to spending the sea days flat out on the lower of these two decks, taking their pillows and deck towels to lie on. After a day or two they decided the decks were too hard and hot to lie on, so late one night they hatched a plan to take a couple of loungers from the Sun Deck down to their favourite spot. This involved carrying two heavy sunbeds furtively down through the ship, along the corridors and out through the forward doors. On the way they must have been spotted by a steward as the following day they found everything had been prepared for them by the crew! The Bridge officers also took to kindly warning them from the Bridge wing when the ship was going to change course and they were going to lose their sun!

Paul Brougham again, 'The Reception Desk had two offices on either side that were occupied by the Deputy Purser and Computer Officer. These offices were each separated from the Reception Desk by identical smoked glass windows. The intention was that the two officers could observe and monitor business at the Reception Desk without being seen themselves. This was only partially successful. The ability to monitor staff at work was too

Above, left and right: A full crew muster drill is held while the ship is berthed at Cadiz, 23 September 2008. The ship's crew are constantly drilled in all emergency procedures, from medical emergencies to the most feared danger at sea – fire. Any fire, however small, results in all passengers being called to their emergency muster stations, while specialist teams deal with the problem. In the other picture, a fire party is practising fire control on the stern deck behind the Conservatory (Lido Café on *Royal Princess*), watched by their officers. (*Sharon Poole & Peter Gibbons*)

Left: The foredeck and bow, pictured from the port bridge wing, on a turnaround day in Southampton, 1 August 2010. These forward observation decks are a wonderful spot to watch an entry into port. Cunard's *Queen Victoria* can be seen ahead, berthed at the Ocean Terminal. (*Sharon Poole*)

The Reception Desk of *Artemis*, with its friendly staff who spotted me taking their photograph! 13 May 2010. (*Sharon Poole*)

great an opportunity to miss when it came to having some fun. We could email messages to the staff on Reception during quieter moments and then we would stand by the glass and watch their reaction. This backfired immediately as we had not noticed that we were visible through the glass when the back office had lights on. We soon learned that in order not to be seen we needed to turn off the office lights and also to close the adjoining door to avoid being heard.'

Many factors can be allowed for, but not every cruise goes to plan. In 1996, *Royal Princess* was on a Baltic Cruise, with an overnight stay in St Petersburg in Russia. Passenger John Ball takes up the story: 'Security on both sides was very strict and Russian Guards patrolled the quayside constantly. The Chief Officer was taking the opportunity of an overnight stop to have part of the hull repainted and two men were suspended on a cradle to do the work. When they finished, the only way down was to lower the cradle and for the men to step into a small boat which landed them on the dockside for them to re-board the ship. The Russian guards promptly arrested them as they stepped off the boat onto the quay and it took a high degree of sweet talking from Commodore Mike Moulin before they were released!'

On 26 April 2001, *Royal Princess* broke her mooring lines while berthed in Port Said, Egypt. As she drifted slowly away from the pier she was side-swiped by a cargo vessel. In November 2003, the opposite happened when she collided with the dockside in one of the Greek Islands, causing a 2.5 metre (8 foot) gash in the bow and delaying departure until repairs were made. As a result, the port of Mykonos had to be cancelled. Passengers had already missed out on Rhodes earlier in the cruise due to sea conditions.

In May 2002, during a transatlantic repositioning cruise, the ship had to turn around and head back towards the Canadian coast so that a sick passenger could be airlifted off and taken to hospital. The ship was one day late arriving in Dover as a result.

Tales of a Ship's Agent

I (Andrew) chatted with my good friend John Peterson of Benfleet, who, in the late 1980s and early 1990s was P&O Containers Ship's Agent in Tilbury. Being all part of the same P&O Group at that time, his job included dealing with the Princess ships berthing at the now renamed London International Cruise Terminal. As Ship's Agent, John was involved in all sorts of problem-solving for passengers and crew alike and recollected some stories of the turnaround days.

John Peterson, P&O Port Agent at Tilbury during the 1990s, pictured on board *Queen Mary 2* in Southampton on a visit in 2007. (*John Peterson*)

Left: Royal Princess and *Crown Odyssey* alongside at Tilbury, 1992. Their shared ancestry is clear from this photograph – both ships were designed by the Danish firm of Knud E. Hansen A/S. *Crown Odyssey* was built in 1988 for Royal Cruise Line (RCL). The following year RCL was sold to Norwegian Cruise Line (NCL) and the ship was renamed *Norwegian Crown*. When NCL bought Orient Lines in 2000, the ship was transferred to their fleet and given her original name back. In September 2003, the lounge area above the bridge was added. In 2006, *Crown Odyssey* was sold to Fred Olsen and renamed *Balmoral*. They took delivery on 7 November 2007 and sent her for a major refit at the Blohm & Voss shipyard in Hamburg, Germany, which included the insertion of a 30 metre (99 foot) midsection, adding 186 passenger and fifty-three crew cabins. Fred Olsen also wanted to remove the lounge area above the bridge, going back to the panoramic lounge below the mast as in the original design, but had to retain it for stability reasons. (*Andrew Sassoli-Walker*)

Below left: Cary Grant with his fifth and last wife, Barbara Harris, on the Riviera Deck with his then cabin steward and stewardess, Stephen Radford and Anne Kelly. At that time, cabin crew worked in pairs so that there was always one person on duty. Cary Grant sailed on *Royal Princess* many times, often joining the officers in the wardroom of an evening, to escape the attention of other passengers. (*Stephen Radford*)

Opposite below right: Senior officers of *Royal Princess* with astronaut Buzz Aldrin, the second man to set foot on the moon, who was on board as a guest speaker.
L-R: Brian Price (Cruise Director), Ken Flavell (First Purser, Food & Beverage), Chris Fuller (Staff Engineer), Trevor Daniel (Chief Engineer), David Harbinson (Staff Electro-Technical Officer), Buzz Aldrin, Emilio Mazzi (First Purser, Admin.), Arturo Calise (Passenger Services Director), Captain Bob Oliver, Steve Mellor (Doctor), Roger Bilton (Staff Captain), Lesley Hockett (Social Hostess). (*David Harbinson*)

Above left: Commodore Mike Moulin with Brenda Jones on board *Royal Princess,* May 2002. Brenda had just won a bottle of champagne for being the passenger who had been sailing for the most number of years. Her first time on board a ship was at the age of 10 when she boarded the RMS *Berengaria* with her mother, brother and sister on 28 July 1928 to sail to New York. Her father had sailed out in February that year on the SS *Leviathan* to take up his new post as manager of a coalmine in Wilkes-Barre, Pennsylvania, and to find accommodation for the family before they joined him. (*Diane Jones*)

Above right: When the news broke of the death of Princess Diana on 31 August 1997, the Public Area Supervisor, Stephen Radford, left a single carnation on the table under her photograph in the Princess Court. By midday, passengers had brought so many flowers from their cabins to add to the floral tribute that a large table was required, then two tables. A Book of Condolence was later added. (*Stephen Radford*)

Above left: *Royal Princess* in dry dock in Norfolk, Virginia, USA, for routine maintenance, November 1997. (*Author's Collection*)

Above right: *Royal Princess* undergoing a refit in the King George V graving dock in Southampton in the mid 1990s. This was the original dry dock built for the *Queen Mary* and *Queen Elizabeth* when Cunard moved their base from Liverpool. (Southern Daily Echo)

Left: The original Princess Seawitch logo on the funnel. The logo was simplified in the mid 1990s by the removal of the eye and the reduction of the number of colours to just blue. (*Andrew Sassoli-Walker*)

Right: Royal Princess berthed at Barcelona, Spain, November 1989. Unusually a lifeboat has been lowered on its davits on the shore side, possibly for maintenance. (*John Blewitt*)

Below left: Royal Princess tendering passengers ashore at Cabo San Lucas, Mexico, 23 May 1985. (*Alan Mackenzie*)

Below right: Royal Princess photographed in the Caribbean from P&O's liner *Canberra*, then on a World Cruise, 25 January 1988. (*Alan Mackenzie*)

Royal Princess swinging on departure from Southampton, and clearly showing off the beautiful tiered stern, something sadly missing from many modern cruise ships today. (Andrew Sassoli-Walker)

the gentle buzz of cleaning and preparing for her new guests. Meanwhile, on the quayside there would be a constant stream of lorries and vans arriving with stores – everything from food and drink, stock for the shops and basic items such as toilet rolls and other necessities. Interestingly, in all the years that *Royal Princess* called at Tilbury, she always left with an even keel draft of 8 metres (26 feet).

John's job also entailed dealing with minor emergencies. One captain had lost a small retaining screw in his spectacles, and in his own words, 'If I don't have them fixed by our departure this evening, I am not sure where we will end up sailing to!' John made a mad dash ashore to the local opticians to get them repaired.

On another turnaround day, a tannoy announcement asked John to head for the Gift Shop. On arrival he was met by a fraught sales lady whose box of gold chain for the famous 'inch of gold' had yet to arrive from Heathrow. She had already gone two round trips with none in stock, and the takings were suffering! With the relevant Air Way Bill in hand, John rang around trying to track down the shipment. Finally, after many calls, the box was located in London. Next problem – how to get it to the ship! A courier was cajoled into collecting the box and riding across London on his day off, arriving at Tilbury with just half an hour to spare before the vessel departed. Following this, John thought he was done for the day and was getting ready to see the ship out on departure, when this now very pleased sales lady said he wasn't leaving until she could give him t-shirts for his children Jenny and Ian, and make-up for his wife Helen! As she disappeared, John was rather hoping that he would be delayed enough to sail with the ship and disembark with the pilot. No such luck, however, and he left the ship to watch another departure from his usual quayside position.

Older ships such as *Canberra* and *QE2* needed at least two tugs, forward and aft, to help them in and out of port. However, *Royal Princess*, with her twin rudders and bow thrusters, was very easy to manoeuvre, although a stern tug was usually required if she needed to turn in a restricted space, either on arrival or departure. Once when John was on leave, he and I (Andrew) were given the opportunity of going out on the Alexander Tug *Sun Mercia* as she assisted *Royal Princess* out of her berth. We made our way over to Gravesend on the Tilbury Ferry *Great Expectations* (now the present Hythe Ferry) to board *Sun Mercia*. At that time she was the biggest tug in the Port of London. Alongside at Tilbury, in addition to the *Royal Princess*, was the Royal Cruise Line ship *Crown Odyssey*, now Fred Olsen's *Balmoral*. It was clear from the silhouettes of both vessels that the same firm of architects, Knud E. Hansen A/S, was involved in the design of both ships. Seeing the departure from this unusual angle and so close up was an impressive sight.

John would be at the terminal in time for the arrival of the ship at 5.15 a.m. Once the gangway was secured, his first job was to meet the ship's officers and, together with Her Majesty's Customs, Port Health and Border Control, get the ship cleared in order for disembarkation to take place. This formal activity and signing of paperwork was usually done over bacon rolls, coffee and tea! Another perk John enjoyed as Agent was the three-course port day lunch which started at 12 noon!

Most passengers had usually disembarked by 10.30 and since most of them were American, they would head straight to either an airport for flights home, or on to hotels in London. Between this time and the commencement of embarkation at 1 p.m., the ship's public areas would be quiet apart from

CHAPTER 5

REBIRTH AND A NEW NAME

In 2005, the year that Princess Cruises celebrated their 40th Anniversary of founding, *Royal Princess* was transferred to the P&O UK fleet in exchange for *Adonia*, which was renamed *Sea Princess*. On 24 May that year, *Royal Princess* sailed into the Lloyd Werft shipyard at Bremerhaven, Germany, for a three-week, £10.5 million transformation into *Artemis*. The new name was appropriately chosen as it is the Greek version of Diana the Huntress, so retaining the ship's special link with HRH The Princess of Wales.

A team of 500 workers began to transform a very American-style ship with large open public areas into a vessel more in keeping with British cruising traditions and tastes. The interior design team was led by interior architect Frank Symeou. His brief was to create a warm cosy feeling, with secluded corners where passengers could relax. Much was retained, such as the striking Spindrift sculpture in the atrium, but complemented with new features such as a stained glass ceiling dome. The fountain at the base of Spindrift was also reinstated after being removed at some point by Princess Cruises who replaced it with a planter. Although aimed at the lover of traditional cruising, there were plenty of modern touches added as well, such as the oriental-themed spa on Deck Nine and the new cyber study.

On the Sun Deck, the lap pool was retiled in order to remove the Princess Seawitch logo that was incorporated into the floor. The Lido Café was extended at the stern over what was an open area of deck with a water feature, and renamed The Conservatory. The small aft serving area that linked the two halves of the Lido Café was removed and two new larger serving areas were installed down each side. The remaining open deck area was furnished with teak tables and chairs and offered 'dining under the stars' when the weather

was appropriate! A new larger bar was built on the Lido Deck, now renamed the Crystal Pool. A plexi-glass enclosure was installed around the pool shower and the tiled surfaces surrounding the smaller pool and whirlpools were given teak decking. The hair-dressing salon was moved up from Deck Two to opposite the spa on Deck Nine, and the space was converted into five new inside cabins that are used for entertainers and lecturers. The two show lounges were retained but an additional overflow dance floor, commonly referred to on board as 'the ashtray', was added in the Riviera Club, which was renamed Starlights. Another change to this lounge was the creation of a wedding chapel in what had once been a secluded area with a spiral staircase up to the Promenade Deck. The Crown Casino, which on *Royal Princess* ran nearly the full width of the ship, was reduced by a third and the space was used for a Cyberstudy (where internet access and computer classes are offered to passengers) and a new separate shop called the Emporium, stocking holiday essentials such as toiletries, batteries, sweets and souvenirs. Probably the biggest change was to the Princess Court piano lounge on Deck Three. What was originally a sitting area with small pantry was turned, with the addition of a cherry-wood bar and chocolate counter, into Tiffany's Bar. As it is at the top of the main stairs down to the Coral Dining Room (the Continental Dining Room under Princess), it is a particularly popular venue for pre-dinner drinks, especially with its large picture windows overlooking the sea. The Library had already been moved twice from its original position outboard of the photo gallery to the midships stair tower on the Promenade Deck, and then back to the Terrace Room when new Safety of Life at Sea (SOLAS) regulations deemed it a fire risk in a stairwell. P&O Cruises kept the Library in the Terrace Room,

Above left: The original crest for *Royal Princess*. The English translation of the Latin motto is 'The Pursuit of Excellence.' (*Andrew Sassoli-Walker*)

Right: The new crest for *Artemis*, painted on the canvas cover over the crew swimming pool. The bow and quiver of arrows is a reference to Artemis being the Greek name for the Roman goddess Diana, the huntress. (*Andrew Sassoli-Walker*)

but the open-plan area was made more intimate with additional bookcases, seating and desks. The decks were renamed after ex-P&O Cruises ships in line with the rest of the fleet. The Sun and Lido decks were unchanged, Aloha became Arcadia, Baja became Britannia, Caribe became Canberra, Dolphin became Promenade Deck, Riviera became Devanha, Plaza became Ellora, and the Main deck became Formosa. In the staterooms, UK power sockets were installed and hospitality trays added so that passengers were able to make their own tea or coffee without having to resort to Room Service. The final touch was to change her name on the bow and stern. The funnel top logo was removed along with the illuminated name on the Sun Deck. The funnel was repainted P&O Cruises buff and an illuminated sign proclaiming her new name was fitted below the mast.

Left: Artemis' ship's bell. This hangs on the foredeck. (*Sharon Poole*)

Above: The helmsman holds up the original brass bell cast with the name *Royal Princess 1984* on the Bridge of *Artemis*, May 2010. (*Sharon Poole*)

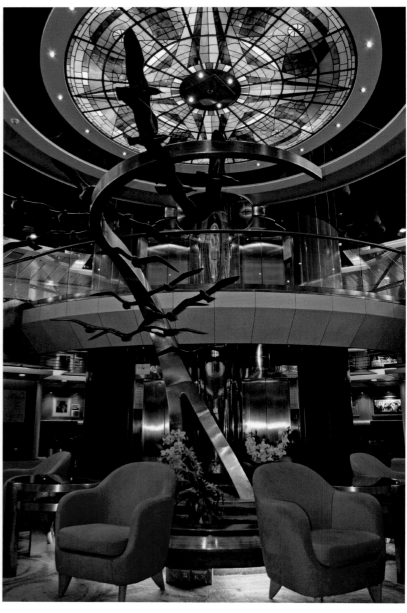

Above left: Portrait of Diana, Princess of Wales, the ship's original godmother, who named *Royal Princess* in November 1984. This hangs in Tiffany's, since the connection was retained when the ship was renamed *Artemis* – the Greek version of the Roman goddess Diana. The framed certificate on the table was the Silver CRUISE award given to *Artemis'* Ship's Company for achieving the position of P&O Ship of the Quarter, 2009. (*Sharon Poole*)

Above right: Spindrift, highlighted by the illuminated stained glass at the ceiling of the Atrium. The latter feature was added by P&O when the ship was refitted as *Artemis*. (*Andrew Sassoli-Walker*)

Above: The Riviera Pool and Bar, pictured on a turnaround day at Southampton, 26 April 2010. (*Sharon Poole*)

Right: A beautiful sunset reflected in the windows of the Conservatory. This part of the terrace is used for 'Dining under the Stars' in appropriate weather. (*Andrew Sassoli-Walker*)

Above left: The Conservatory, being laid for that evening's themed dinner, 16 January 2006. (*Carlos Price*)

Above right: Early in the morning at sea in May 2010, and the ship stirs into life. Decks have been washed down, hand rails wiped of the salt deposits and the sun beds neatly laid out ready for use. The atmosphere on board imperceptibly changes as the winds drop and the sun comes out. Passengers begin to appear, firstly in ones and twos with cameras and binoculars, before the rush of sun-worshippers. The regimented lines of sun beds are pushed and pulled into a jumble, blocking stairs and gangways as people stake their claim to a sunny piece of deck. (*Sharon Poole*)

Left: Starlights Lounge. Dancing is popular on P&O ships and this 'overflow' dance floor was added to what was the Riviera Club when *Royal Princess* was converted into *Artemis*. It is colloquially referred to on board as The Ashtray! (*Sharon Poole*)

Above left: Wedding chapel, featuring a skylight and spiral staircase. In her days as *Royal Princess*, this was a secluded part of the Riviera Club with access to the Promenade Deck via the staircase, but when P&O refitted the ship as *Artemis*, the space lent itself to conversion as an elegant wedding venue with the addition of fabric screening from the main part of Starlights Lounge. (*Sharon Poole*)

Above right: The glitz of the Monte Carlo Casino, 13 June 2010. (*Andrew Sassoli-Walker*)

Right: Tiffany's Bar, June 2010. This is situated midships, on Deck Three. Originally this was the Princess Court piano lounge. It was fitted with a bar and chocolate counter when P&O Cruises acquired the ship in 2005 and it is a popular place for pre-dinner cocktails as lifts and stairs lead down from here to the main Atrium and entrance to the Coral Dining Room. (*Sharon Poole*)

Above: A reminder of *Artemis'* previous life as *Royal Princess.* A deck name plate has fallen off this lift control revealing Aloha Deck instead of Arcadia Deck. (*Sharon Poole*)

Above left: Part of the 700-book library with librarian Prasana Reddy, 1 August 2010. As well as books, newspapers and magazines, there are also DVDs available for the suites and mini-suites. (*Sharon Poole*)

Below left: The starboard side corridor with the library to the right and Starlights lounge ahead, 1 August 2010. An atlas is displayed at the entrance to the Library, open at the appropriate page for the location of the ship. (*Andrew Sassoli-Walker*)

Above left The Illuminated name of the oldest ship in the P&O Cruises Fleet. (*Andrew Sassoli-Walker*)

Above right: Captain David Pembridge watching with actress Prunella Scales as the bottle of champagne smashes against the stern superstructure and *Royal Princess* is officially renamed *Artemis*, 16 June 2005. (*P&O Cruises*)

Right: Ticker tape and streamers are released as actress Prunella Scales names *Artemis*, 16 June 2005. This was the first time a ship has been named while at sea. On the left are master of ceremonies Sir Trevor McDonald and master of the ship Captain David Pembridge. On the right is David Dingle, then managing director and now Chief Executive of P&O Cruises' parent company, Carnival UK. (*P&O Cruises*)

Next page: Artemis' Naming Day Programme and Luncheon Menu, 16 June 2005. (*John Sutherland*)

When completed, *Artemis* was recognisably a P&O Cruises ship, with elements of some of the most popular vessels in the fleet. The corridors along the main deck are outboard like those on the current *Oriana*, with a passenger flow similar to the second *Arcadia* (built as *Star Princess*, currently sailing as *Ocean Village* but soon to depart for P&O Australia under her new name, *Pacific Pearl*) with lots of natural light and informal sitting areas.

On 13 June 2005, *Artemis* arrived at the Mayflower Terminal in Southampton ready for her management inspection, crew induction and preparations for another first – a naming at sea! She was going on a special cruise down the Solent to the Isle of Wight, where invited guests would spend a luxurious day at Osborne House, once home to Queen Victoria and Prince Albert, before sailing home again. The naming ceremony would be performed en route.

On Thursday 16 June, the Royal Marines Band played for the guests as they arrived at the terminal and boarded *Artemis*. Her lines were slipped and she slowly edged into the river, ticker tape flying from her sides as the band played 'Rule Britannia'. Presiding over the order of ceremonies was television journalist and newsreader Sir Trevor McDonald OBE, who commented that what he liked about a naming ceremony was that it was both glamorous

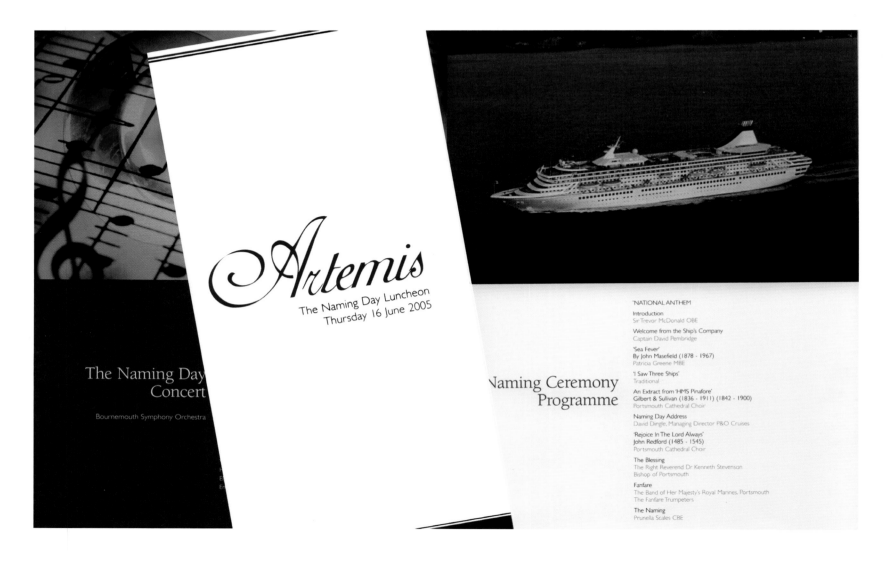

The Naming Day
Concert

Bournemouth Symphony Orchestra

Artemis

The Naming Day Luncheon
Thursday 16 June 2005

Naming Ceremony
Programme

'NATIONAL ANTHEM

Introduction
Sir Trevor McDonald OBE

Welcome from the Ship's Company
Captain David Pembridge

'Sea Fever'
By John Masefield (1878 - 1967)
Patricia Greene MBE

'I Saw Three Ships'
Traditional

An Extract from 'HMS Pinafore'
Gilbert & Sullivan (1836 - 1911) (1842 - 1900)
Portsmouth Cathedral Choir

Naming Day Address
David Dingle, Managing Director P&O Cruises

'Rejoice In The Lord Always'
John Redford (1485 - 1545)
Portsmouth Cathedral Choir

The Blessing
The Right Reverend Dr Kenneth Stevenson
Bishop of Portsmouth

Fanfare
The Band of Her Majesty's Royal Marines, Portsmouth
The Fanfare Trumpeters

The Naming
Prunella Scales CBE

and traditional, much like the ship herself. The guests assembled at the stern where the Portsmouth Cathedral Choir stood on one side and the Royal Marines Band the other. Actress Patricia Greene (Jill Archer in *The Archers* radio show) began by reading the poem *Sea Fever* by John Masefield. The Bishop of Portsmouth, the Right Reverend Dr Kenneth Stevenson then said a prayer for the ship before handing over to *Artemis'* new Godmother, actress Prunella Scales, to perform the naming. As she cut the ribbon, the magnum of champagne swung free against the superstructure and silver streamers flew through the air. Once ashore at Osborne House, the guests took part in a day of time-honoured English summer activities, with afternoon tea on the terraces, tours of the house, and at 7 p.m., a champagne picnic supper on the Durbar Lawn accompanied by music from the Bournemouth Symphony Orchestra conducted by Gavin Sutherland. The climax of the day was a firework display lighting up the night sky.

The following day, *Artemis* sailed on her maiden voyage under the P&O Cruises flag to the Baltic Capitals under the command of Captain David Pembridge.

CHAPTER 6

THE P&O CRUISES YEARS 2005-2011

From the beginning, *Artemis* was marketed as the explorer of the fleet with a move away from the usual itineraries, offering several longer voyages of three and four weeks each. *Artemis* was especially welcomed by those P&O Cruises passengers who had enjoyed the small-ship experience on *Victoria*, and had had no equivalent vessel since that ship was sold in 2002. Although twice the size of *Victoria*, at 45,000 tons *Artemis* was almost half the size of the next smallest ship – the 76,000 ton *Oriana*.

Over her years in service, *Artemis* has sailed in every major ocean and to around 290 of the world's most well-known and more out-of-the-way ports. Her smaller size allows her to operate more adventurous itineraries off the beaten track. For example, in 2006 she sailed on a thirty-eight-night cruise up the Amazon and Orinoco Rivers. Instead of the normal world cruises, each year she sailed on a Grand Odyssey. In 2008, this took her right around South America, rounding Cape Horn. Her final Grand Voyage in 2011 will be a ninety-eight-night cruise to Africa, Asia, and the Orient. In the Mediterranean she has called at Sorrento and St Raphael; in Scandinavia she has sailed among the Lofoten Islands; and in the Baltic Sea she has visited Vaasa in Finland and Klaipeda in Lithuania! She has cruised north to Greenland and south to Antarctica; to the Black Sea, Lebanon, Costa Rica and China.

These exotic itineraries have proved very popular with passengers although they can present their own diverse range of problems. Extracts from some of the cruise logs over the years have a certain understated comment!

Monday 30 July 2007 Gothab, Greenland … The starboard anchor was aweigh at 17.54 and by 18.01 was home. Various courses were set to retrace our route back out into the Labrador Sea. Once clear we set various southerly courses towards Julienhab.

Tuesday 31 July 2007. A series of south-easterly courses were set towards Julienhab in Greenland … Conditions: Overcast with dense fog patches.

Wednesday 1 August 2007 … Due to the huge amount of ice and restricted visibility our stop in Julienhab was cancelled as it was deemed unsafe … the port … was completely surrounded by large icebergs.

Captain Box later told passengers that one of the icebergs the ship passed in the night was the size of a skyscraper, but that although it was quite a sight to behold, he thought better of announcing it through the ship's tannoy system in case of frightening everyone!

The Captain is of course not only responsible for the safety of the ship, but every crew member and passenger on board. In many ports, passengers are ferried to shore in the ship's tenders. It may be calm and serene in the morning when the ship anchors, but a careful watch has to be kept on the weather and sea in case conditions deteriorate. As Jane Bristow reported from a Round Britain cruise in August 2010, 'Yesterday was Lerwick. We had a fabulous morning there and we could have been in the Mediterraenan. However, things quickly changed. The weather deteriorated and getting out of the tenders to get back on to the ship was quite scary!' The tenders also double up as lifeboats and the ship cannot sail off leaving one behind. This was a cruise log report for a call at Sochi in Russia in 2008: 'Friday 12 September 2008. During the early hours of the morning *Artemis* continued to cruise along the north coast of Turkey heading north towards Sochi.

Billed as the explorer of the fleet, *Artemis* is photographed among icebergs on part of her South American Odyssey, 2008. This was Food & Beverage Manager Jo Haxby's favourite voyage. The ship left Southampton for the Caribbean, then sailed up the Amazon before rounding Cape Horn to Chile and back via the Panama Canal. She described her amazement at seeing icebergs so large they had their own cloud formations! (*The Ship's Photographer*)

Above: Artemis at Stavanger, Norway, 9 August 2007. The Gamla Stavanger is the oldest part of the town, filled with narrow cobbled streets and wooden houses. One of the two cruise ship berths is right next to this attractive scene. (*Sharon Poole*)

Above left: Artemis berthed alongside fleet sister *Oceana* at Tortola in the British Virgin Islands, 10 November 2009. (*Peter Gibbons*)

Left: Artemis at Reykjavik, Iceland, 3 August 2007. This cruise was dogged by bad weather and missed ports. After leaving Southampton on 24 July, the first port should have been Glengariff in Ireland two days later, but the seas were too high to run the tender operation. Following its next port, Nuuk in Greenland, was supposed to be Qaqortoq, but the harbour was unseasonably still full of ice, so the ship headed for Reykjavik. On arrival, high winds kept *Artemis* off her berth until midday, so another half a day of sightseeing was lost to passengers. On leaving Reykjavik, the next scheduled stop was Akureyri in Iceland, but heavy seas and overnight fog delayed *Artemis* and so another port of call had to be cancelled. The decks were closed and passengers were asked to stay in their cabins initially. The ship reached Alesund in Norway on 6 August and from then on it was a completely different cruise with sunny skies and calm seas all the way down the coast of Norway and back to Southampton on 11 August. (*Sharon Poole*)

Above left: Artemis alongside at the Norwegian port of Eidfjord on 4 August 2010, dwarfed by the towering mountains that surround the fjord. (*Jeanette Fluellen*)

Above right: Artemis moored alongside at Eidfjord, Norway in glorious weather, August 2007. (*Peter Dutton*)

Left: Artemis at Oslo, Norway, 9 December 2007. This was one of the ports on her Winter Wonderland Christmas Markets cruise that year. She was guided to the berth in the morning darkness by a row of flaming torch lights, lit by a man walking along the dockside. As *Artemis* tied up under the ramparts of the fourteenth-century Akerhus Castle, it began to snow, making the whole experience quite magical. (*Sharon Poole*)

Opposite: In her final year with P&O Cruises, *Artemis* makes her maiden call at Greencastle, Northern Ireland, as part of a Norway and Iceland cruise, 13 August 2010. (*Jeanette Fluellen*)

Above left: Artemis on her maiden visit to the Clyde, with the iconic paddle-steamer *Waverley* sailing past full of sightseers, 8 September 2009. *Waverley* was built in 1947 and is the last sea-going paddle-steamer surviving in the world. (*Lesley Wild*)

Above right: Artemis leaves Rosyth (for excursions to Edinburgh) as part of a Round Britain Cruise in her farewell year, August 2010. She is about to pass under the distinctive Forth Rail Bridge. This is an engineering masterpiece completed 120 years ago and still carrying over 180 trains a day over the Firth of Forth. (*Jim Simpson*)

Left: Artemis arrives at Nessebur in Bulgaria as dawn breaks in the Black Sea, September 2010. Unfortunately, despite looking reasonably calm, the swell was too great for the required tendering operation and the port had to be cancelled. (*Sharon Poole*)

Artemis drifting in the caldera at Santorini, pictured from one of the shore tenders used to ferry passengers to the landing stage, September 2008. This Greek island has been shaped by the largest volcanic eruption of recent geological times. In around 1600 BC the residents of Santorini fled in advance of a huge explosion that wiped out most of the civilization in Greece at the time. It is probably the root of the Atlantis legend. The caldera is too deep for any ship to anchor, so they maintain their relative position by the use of their engines, while passengers are tendered ashore. (*Sharon Poole*)

Left: Lowering the tenders to take passengers ashore at Cannes, France, 10 May 2010. (*Sharon Poole*)

Below left: Tendering passengers ashore at Cannes in the south of France, 10 May 2010. (*Sharon Poole*)

Below right: Artemis' tender at the landing stage in Cannes, France, 10 May 2010. The contrast between the tender and the luxury private yachts (in port for the Cannes Film Festival) is somewhat marked, but on the other hand, we were able to indulge ourselves in a little 'Our boat (*Artemis*) is bigger than yours' banter! (*Sharon Poole*)

Artemis alongside at Palma, Majorca, May 2010. (*Sharon Poole*)

Artemis refuelling in Piraeus after a seven-day-straight sail from Southampton, May 2010. During this time she was running on just three engines while ship's engineers attempted to repair the fourth with assistance from staff from the Pielstick factory in France, makers of the original engine. (*Sharon Poole*)

Right: Artemis at Istanbul, Turkey, September 2008. The stern decks are a lovely place to sit when at sea as they are sheltered from any wind. They also provide excellent views of any port. The oval plaque, centre right, is one of the two Wärtsilä builder's plates. (*Sharon Poole*)

Below left: Artemis moored in Kusudasi in Turkey on 6 May 2010. The American warship is the USS *Ramage* DDG 61, an Arleigh Burke-class Guided Missile Destroyer. She carries a crew of twenty-two officers and 300 enlisted men. (*Sharon Poole*)

Below right: Artemis riding at anchor off Nuuk (or in Danish – Gothab) in Greenland, 30 July 2007. Sailing in this region has its dangers and a specialised ice pilot was on board to assist in navigating *Artemis* through the thick fogs and Arctic ice which was still evident even in midsummer. On the approach to Nuuk, *Artemis* was surrounded by floating ice and small bergs (growlers and bergy bits). These small chunks of ice, rising about a metre (3 feet) out of the water can still be dangerous to shipping because they are harder to spot than large icebergs. (*Sharon Poole*)

We reached the anchor position as recommended by the port and dropped anchor at 06.42. The tenders were launched into the water but due to confused swell of about 1.5 metres making the operation unsafe the Captain in consultation with his senior officers decided to recover the tenders back on board and cancel the call at this port.' The recovery operation alone took well over one hour.

Unfortunately, accidents and illness are no respecters of holidays. To cater for such events, the ship is well equipped with four one- and two-bed wards, two consultation rooms, x-ray equipment, an intensive care unit and treatment room. I (Sharon) had first-hand experience of the latter when I managed to trip on the cobbled granite quayside at Copenhagen, breaking my glasses and requiring stitches to my forehead.

Unlike in her Princess days, the stairs from the Promenade Deck up to the forward observation decks are accessible to passengers and these are wonderful spots to watch an entry into port. I (Sharon) will never forget the day we sailed into the harbour at Nuuk, Greenland, in 2007. As I was standing there alone, watching the ship sail through the many small islands and chunks of ice (growlers), a humpback whale spouted and then slowly lifted its tail and dived. It was utter magic, as was an early evening sail up the Bosphorus from Istanbul to the Black Sea, with the setting sun reflected in the windows of the palaces lining the Asian side of this ancient waterway.

Comings and goings are always interesting to watch, but never more so than on a maiden call at a port. I (Andrew) was on board in 2008 on Artemis' first visit to Amsterdam since being renamed. After an overnight stay in port, our departure was made extra special with a water display from fireboats which escorted Artemis away from her berth. This was accompanied by lots of whistle blowing by Artemis and other vessels in reply.

Early morning at Sochi, Russia, September 2008. Unfortunately there was a heavy confused swell and the decision was made to abandon the tendering operation. It took over an hour to recover all the boats and set sail for the next port of Yalta in Ukraine on this Black Sea cruise. (*Sharon Poole*)

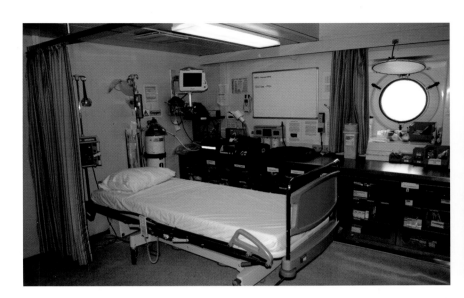

Above left: The one part of the ship that everyone hopes they will not see – the intensive care unit in the Medical Centre on Deck Zero. The medical facilities include a waiting room, two consulting rooms, three one- and two-bed wards and intensive care unit. Similar facilities are also provided for crew members.
(*Andrew Sassoli-Walker*)

Above right: The forward observation decks are a popular place to watch entries into ports, or as here, an evening sail up the Bosphorus from Istanbul to the Black Sea, September 2008. (*Sharon Poole*)

Right: A majestic *Artemis*, looking her best on an overnight stay at Amsterdam. September 2008. (*Andrew Sassoli-Walker*)

Above: Officers 'wave' from the bridge wing to the *Grand Holiday* (ex-*Carnival Holiday*) at Barcelona, Spain, 11 May 2010. (*Sharon Poole*)

Below: Captain David Box (arms outstretched) berths *Artemis* at Amsterdam with assistance from the local pilot, September 2008. (*Andrew Sassoli-Walker*)

Around the same time that *Artemis* joined the fleet, the New Horizons programme was introduced on the two child-free ships, *Arcadia* and *Artemis*. The idea was that, along with the familiar daytime activities such as shuffleboard tournaments, bridge, lectures and so on, a new programme of workshops, classes and talks would allow passengers to develop new skills, taught by experts and guest speakers. On *Artemis*, the subjects included political and maritime history, British architecture, painting, jewellery making, floristry, classical music and literature.

In December 2007, *Artemis* had two weeks in dry dock in Bremerhaven for a complete refit involving an interior makeover and the application of a new fuel-efficient hull coating. Six new balcony staterooms were also created, utilising the midships lounge areas on A, B and C Decks, incorporating the public balconies on A deck and creating similar balconies on the two lower decks. The Deck Nine Horizon Lounge showed the greatest change, with a yachting theme introduced along with new contemporary dark wood furniture and comfortable sofas. The bar was completely re-modelled and the wooden dance floor moved to allow for additional seating. New plasma television screens were fitted to show news and sports channels and an up-to-date sound and lighting system was installed for when the lounge becomes a night club in the late evening.

Most of the carpeting and soft furnishings were renewed throughout the ship, including those in Starlights and the Coral Dining Room. As well as new soft furnishings, Trumps card room was given new baize-topped tables. One of the more artistically minded night staff took to brushing a design into the nap of these tables each night. It even reached the point where passengers were getting up early to go into the room before Bridge classes began to see what design had been produced that day – dolphins, fish, birds, or flowers!

The Conservatory was given new carpets, blinds and upholstery in a fresh new colour scheme of oranges, browns and yellows, all of which co-ordinated with the new table tops and natural wood-effect flooring in the food serving area. Around the Crystal Pool, new canopies and equipment for coloured lighting effects were installed, which transformed the deck area and gave it a new more interesting ambience for evening events.

In the cabins, the mattresses were renewed and bedding changed from sheets and blankets to duvets, although the former were still available at the request of passengers. At the same time, new runners and scatter cushions were added and bathrooms were refreshed with re-tiling, new taps and fittings. The changes were not just to the physical fabric of the ship. As part of the new P&O Cruises Elevation Programme, a new champagne breakfast menu was introduced, along with more gala dinners, an improved wine list, greater choice of therapies in the spa and new shore excursions.

Left: An impressive view of *Artemis'* bow while she was in dry dock at Bremerhaven, April 2010. The bulbous bow at the bottom modifies the way the water flows around the hull, reducing drag and thus increasing speed, range, fuel efficiency, and stability. (*The Ship's Photographer*)

Above: Six new balcony staterooms were added during the refit in December 2007. These were installed in the midships stair tower on A, B and C Decks. (*Sharon Poole*)

Above, left and right: The Horizon Lounge, 13 June 2010. Following the refit in December 2007, the dance floor was moved to create a larger seating area. At the same time a new yachting theme was introduced with new chairs and sofas, and a lighter colour scheme. (*Sharon Poole & Andrew Sassoli-Walker*)

Left: Starlights Lounge with its large wooden dance floor. On the back wall is one of the original tufted wool artworks designed specially for *Royal Princess* in 1984. (*Andrew Sassoli-Walker*)

The International Lounge, 2010. The painted mixed-media panels are part of the original art work commissioned for *Royal Princess* in 1984. Compare photo with that on page 49. (*Andrew Sassoli-Walker*)

Entrance to the Coral Dining Room, with the badge of the Gastronomic Society Chaine des Rotisseurs of which P&O Cruises are members. Every Executive Chef is inducted into this body, which ensures each ship of the fleet features a member on board at all times. (*Andrew Sassoli-Walker*)

Right: The Coral Dining Room, set for dinner, 1 August 2010 (*Andrew Sassoli-Walker*)

Below left: Dining table set for the Tropical Night dinner, 6 May 2010. (*Sharon Poole*)

Below right: Night worker Nixon Fernandes with some of the designs he produces each night on the baize card table surfaces in Trumps. He does this by carefully brushing the nap, often using toothbrushes to achieve the fine detail. It should be said that this was his idea and is not a P&O requirement!

Above left: The Conservatory buffet restaurant, following the 2007 refit. The whole area was refurbished with new flooring, table tops and upholstery. (*Sharon Poole*)

Above right: The aft end of the Conservatory, 13 June 2010. Originally, this was the servery area and was a little smaller. In 2005, P&O enlarged this part by building over part of the aft deck and by moving the serveries to each side of the area, creating a more spacious restaurant with more seating. (*Andrew Sassoli-Walker*)

Left: Artemis overnights at Amsterdam on her maiden call at the Dutch capital. The new coloured lighting around the Crystal Pool is shown to advantage here. (*Andrew Sassoli-Walker*)

Superior Deluxe Balcony Stateroom A351. This is one of six additional staterooms created in December 2007 within the midships lounge areas on A, B and C decks. (*P&O Cruises*)

Above left: The Canberra Suite, one of the two 806 square feet Royal suites on board. These feature a Jacuzzi bath, curtained-off bedroom area (with views of the sea when the curtains are open) and separate sitting and dining areas. The painting on the wall is of the SS *Canberra*, after whom the suite is named. In 1984, these suites cost on average around $600 per person per day, at double occupancy. The average US salary then was $16,000 a year – the cost of a two week cruise for two in this stateroom. (*Andrew Sassoli-Walker*)

Above right: A view of twin cabin C115, with Diane Jones on the fold down bed. Compare this photograph with the one of the same cabin in 1989 when the ship was sailing as *Royal Princess* (p.50). (*Andrew Sassoli-Walker*)

In addition to constantly updating the ship in line with customer expectations, behind the scenes the machinery of the ship has the same treatment, not only to improve efficiency, but to comply with increasingly stringent environmental controls and stricter guidelines by such bodies as the International Maritime Organisation's MARPOL (Marine Pollution), and the US Coast Guard. In many cases both *Artemis* and the rest of the fleet exceed these regulations. Whenever a ship calls in the United States, the Authorities score a ship with marks out of a hundred for cleanliness. Any ship that scores below eighty-five is considered not satisfactory. *Artemis* on her last report scored a very respectable ninety-three.

Fuel consumption remains good, even though the ship is the oldest in the P&O Cruises fleet. This is probably because she was designed to be fuel efficient from the start and to burn the lowest grade of fuel oil. Staff Chief Engineer Paul Yeoman confirmed this, telling us that over an average of twenty-four hours, 114 tonnes is used when all four engines are in use with the ship travelling at her maximum speed of twenty-two knots (normal cruising speed is twenty knots).

As one walks around the outer decks, a strange intermittent compressor noise can often be heard. Soot deposits and the high temperatures in the exhaust area can lead to a fire, so a device called an Intonating Soot Removal System is fitted. To put it simply, it is similar to an air horn, and the pressure of the device shakes free any deposits, removing them from the lining of the exhausts from the main engine, boiler and incinerator.

The Chief Engineer heads up a department of nineteen officers and forty-six crew. The officers can be identified on board by the purple in their shoulder stripes. This is the Royal purple, worn with permission of King George V from 1912 onwards, after the sinking of the *Titanic*. It is in recognition of the fact that no engineering officers survived because they stayed at their posts endeavouring to keep the lights on and control the flooding as long as possible to aid the evacuation of passengers.

Top left: Engineer Stan Konev supervising fitters replacing an overhauled main engine piston and connecting rod. They are guiding the piston and rod into the cylinder bore while it is slowly lowered on the engine room crane.

Above left: Honing of a cylinder liner bore, 6 October 2008. When an engine has been running for some time, the side thrust from the pistons wear the cylinder liners oval. During overhaul the cylinder liners are measured for wear and ovality. If the liners are slightly oval they can be brought back to concentric by using a honing machine which rotates with abrasive stones pressing on the cylinder's sides while it is lowered up and down its length. It also breaks the polished glaze worn onto the cylinder liner surface and gives the correct roughness for lubricating oil to adhere to and help run in new piston rings.

Above right: Crew members climbing up the funnel to rig fairy lights for an overnight stay in Istanbul, 7 September 2008. (*Sharon Poole*)

Fresh from her last, and unscheduled, refit under P&O Cruises, *Artemis* gleams alongside the City Cruise Terminal, Southampton, April 2010. Behind her at the Mayflower Terminal is fleet sister *Aurora*. (*Andrew Sassoli-Walker*)

ARTEMIS Fifth Anniversary Celebration 16th June 2010

Captain Sarah Breton with most of the passengers, around the Crystal Pool on the occasion of *Artemis'* fifth birthday with P&O Cruises. (*The Ship's Photographer*)

In 2009, *Artemis* celebrated her silver anniversary; twenty-five years of taking passengers across the globe. She has remained a popular ship with most voyages fully booked and a high number of repeat cruisers.

It was unfortunate that the first six months of service in 2010 (her final full year under P&O Cruises) were marred by a persistent engine problem that defied several attempts to rectify. An unscheduled two-week refit was urgently fitted in and *Artemis* sailed to the Lloyd Werft yard in Bremerhaven on 4 April 2010. While she was in the yard, the opportunity was also taken to do additional work including steel repairs, extensive pipe repairs, maintenance work on the propulsion plant, stabilizers and bow thrusters, and repainting of the hull above and below the waterline. The inspection revealed that the engine problem required a lot more than just a major service, and was not going to be rectified during her yard time. While the ship returned to her scheduled programme of cruises, specially machined engine parts were made in France at the Pielstick factory, where the original engines were designed. These were flown out to the ship, along with factory engineers to assist the on-board department in fitting them. However, when the engine was run up to full speed again, the bearings overheated and resulted in a further shutdown.

The consequent reduction of speed meant missed ports and a lot of unhappy passengers. The problem was finally resolved in June with the fitting of four additional new parts and much hard work by the engineering department, all done while the ship was at sea. Following these problems, the ship was nominated for the Silver CRUISE award by P&O Cruises. This is a scheme whereby staff members are nominated by fellow crew and/or passengers for going the extra mile and providing service above and beyond that expected of them. The award came with the following citation, '*Artemis*, despite major technical challenges which resulted in enormous pressure on the technical team and compromises to itinerary. In conjunction with their colleagues ashore, the team on board have worked tirelessly to resolve the technical issues and to maintain an excellent product for our passengers. The team really pulled together to deliver results in testing circumstances. Truly excellent, well done Artemis.'

On 16 June 2010, *Artemis* celebrated her fifth birthday under the P&O Cruises flag. Midway through a Mediterranean cruise a special party was held on the Riviera Deck, where the captain and as many passengers who could squeeze in had their photo taken to commemorate the event.

Previous page: The complete crew complement as of April 2010, pictured at the side of the Crystal Pool. They are arranged in their job groups with, from the left at the top: Engineering Department, Deck Officers, Security staff and entertainers. From the left at the bottom: cabin crew, food and beverage staff and the hotel department. (*The Ship's Photographer*)

The original *Royal Princess* bell complete with marine chart of Southampton (her home port for many of her years), officer's cap, binoculars, parallel rule, etc., laid out on the chart table on the Bridge. (*Andrew Sassoli-Walker*)

Tales from below stairs!

It strikes me (Sharon) that a cruise ship is very much like the proverbial swan, with a public face of calm and elegance, but with the crew working hard in the background. I chatted to some of the departmental heads on a three-week Mediterranean cruise in 2010. Without fail all of them commented on what a happy ship *Artemis* is to work on, with a caring, family atmosphere among the crew. They work long hours, but also have a lot of fun off duty.

In April 2010, *Artemis* hit the headlines when Sarah Breton was promoted to Captain and Master of *Artemis*, becoming only the second woman in the world to command a major cruise liner and the first for P&O Cruises. The first was the Swede Karin Stahre Janson, who took charge of the US ship, *Monarch of the Seas* for Royal Caribbean Cruise International in 2007. 'It really does fulfil a lifelong ambition of mine to be a captain,' said Sarah, who added that her maiden voyage at the helm will be even more special because *Artemis,* or rather *Royal Princess* as she was at the time, was the first cruise

ship she ever served on after joining P&O Cruises. Captain Breton has spent upwards of seven years on and off working on this ship. She first joined *Royal Princess* as Third Officer in 1989 when P&O were, for the first time, recruiting deck officers outside of their own cadetships. She then spent time on *Canberra* before returning to *Royal Princess*. Over the years she has held every single deck position: Fourth, Third and Second Officers, Senior Second Officer, First Officer (Navigator), Safety Officer, Staff Captain, and finally in April 2010 she was promoted to the rank of Captain and given command of *Artemis*. Naturally in all that time she has developed a fondness for the ship and made some good friends among the officers. She also remarked on what an excellent ship *Artemis* is on which to learn seamanship. Without the stern thrusters found on all modern ships, officers need to take weather and wind conditions into greater account, particularly when arriving or departing from a berth.

Above left: Ship's wheel on the Bridge. This might be a disappointment to those who might assume ships are still steered by large wooden wheels! Many of the newest cruise liners do not have a wheel at all anymore. To the far right are the engine controls and between those and the wheel are the joysticks for the bow thrusters. (*Sharon Poole*)

Above right: The Bridge showing the communications and navigation desk – compare this with the photo of the same area taken on sea trials (p.27). (*Andrew Sassoli-Walker*)

Right: Artemis' Bridge status board, 13 June 2010. This board shows at a glance the mooring, bunkering and discharge arrangements, whether the swimming pools are filled or empty, whether the captain and staff captain are ashore and to-do lists among other vital information. (*Andrew Sassoli-Walker*)

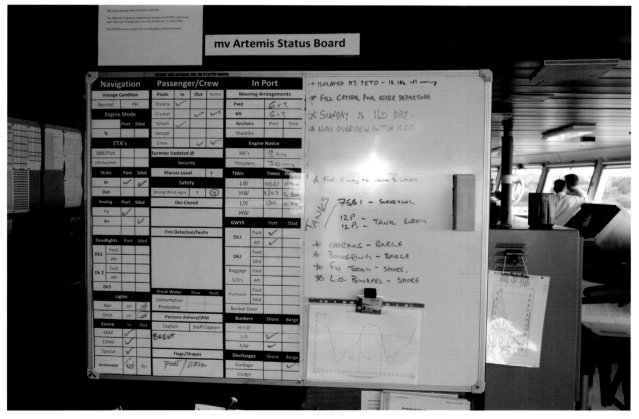

Left: Captain Sarah Breton on the Bridge, looking at photos for an early draft of this book, when the authors paid a visit to the ship on 13 June 2010. (*Sharon Poole*)

Below: Captain Sarah Breton and Deputy Captain Steve Howarth with the local pilot on the bridge wing of *Artemis*, leaving Istanbul, Turkey, 5 May 2010. The pilot was so proud to be on the first UK passenger ship to be commanded by a woman, he insisted on a photograph being taken of himself with the Captain. (*Sharon Poole*)

A few admitted they had initial reservations about being assigned to the oldest ship in the fleet, but soon changed their minds on arrival. Executive Purser Zak Coombs remembers the moment about two or three days after joining the ship in 2005. He was leaving the Coral Dining Room after the first formal dinner and looked up at the stained glass ceiling in Tiffany's. He noted the lights, the colour, the sweeping staircases, the beautiful Spindrift sculpture with its fountain, the sound of the piano drifting down from above, and all the passengers in black ties and evening gowns, and it took his breath away. 'I was hooked, there and then, by the magic of *Artemis*.' His later comment sums her up equally well, 'She is as big as *Canberra* with the intimacy of *Victoria*,' both much-loved ex-P&O Cruises ships. 'The frequent passengers speak of that indefinable thing that draws them back to us time and time again. That is what they like, the friendliness of the ship. It is wonderful to be able to find the time to wander around the ship during the day and to meet so many passengers one knows from previous ships and previous visits to *Artemis*. Being a smaller ship you bump into people when walking about the parish so you keep up to speed with what they are doing, where they have been and how they are enjoying their cruise – it is like old friends keeping in touch. We have raised lots of money for charities, having the Big Tea Party for SSAFA, a Children-in-Need day and a charity day for Operation Smile where we raised around £5,000. At the time of writing (August 2010) the crew are preparing for a big fund raiser in aid of the Pakistan Disaster Relief Fund. Suffice to say I am pleased to be here now and happy to have had a chance to be part of the success story that is the "Little Ship with a Big Heart". I will miss her when she has gone but I am very proud and VERY happy to have been part of the *Artemis* story.'

Stephen Radford, currently Accommodation Manager with thirty-seven years service with P&O Cruises, was another who cut his teeth on *Canberra*. He joined *Royal Princess* as cabin steward and was one of many who were shown over the ship while she was still in the dockyard in Helsinki in 1984. His first impression, again, was that she was similar in size to *Canberra*, but bright and modern with striking artworks and lots of colour. It was the beginning of the commercial age of cruising and here was new inspiration for a new age at a time when the older ships were sometimes thought of as old-fashioned and traditional. One of the main differences on *Royal Princess* from a crew perspective was that they were never more than two to a cabin, each of which had an en-suite bathroom. After the communal showers of *Canberra* this was luxury indeed, although Stephen comments that a certain degree of camaraderie was lost by this. To compensate they took to leaving their cabin doors open so people could stop and chat when passing. Nothing was ever stolen or borrowed (save maybe the odd drop of gin!). There is a great social life for those that work on board. *Artemis* has a crew bar, crew library, crew gym, even a pool of communal bicycles for use in ports. They have their own club, and quizzes and raffles are held to raise money, which is then used for a party or barbeque in port. At the stern on Deck Two is an open area reserved for crew use only, with a small swimming pool and space for gatherings, etc. There is a diverse range of nationalities among the crew and everyone's religious and national holidays are observed on board, with appropriate celebrations and ethnic food. Almost half the ship's company, 241 to be precise, work in the food and beverage department. This number includes everyone from the person who washes dishes, through the waiters and bar stewards up to the Executive Chef and Food & Beverage Manager. There are also crew sporting teams – basketball, running, football, cycling, table tennis, darts, carom (an Indian board game), and even fishing, especially up in Norway and Iceland. These teams are extremely successful, competing against locals or crew members from other ships in such tournaments as the Seven Seas Football Tournament, the Mediterranean Cup, the Nordic Cup or the Bergen Cruise Ship Cup. In 2010,

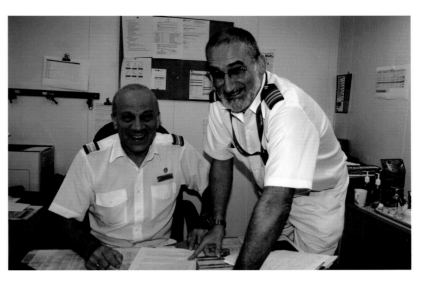

Accommodation Manager Stephen Radford (left) with Executive Purser Zak Coombs, 13 June 2010. Stephen joined the ship originally in 1984, as cabin steward. Zak joined her in 2005 when she was transferred to P&O Cruises from Princess. Between them they have over seventy years service with P&O and both have been on *Artemis* on and off since 2005 when she joined the P&O Cruises fleet. (*Andrew Sassoli-Walker*)

the *Artemis* crew beat those from the *Queen Victoria* at football by 2 goals to 0 in Bergen, Norway. Considering the size of ship, and thus smaller pool of people to draw on, their wins are an even greater achievement.

Jo Haxby, Food and Beverage Manager, also joined *Artemis* in 2005 when the ship was transferred from Princess. Jo found that maintenance of some of the galley equipment was a challenge at first. Unlike many cruise lines operating today, on P&O Cruises ships all the food, including bread and sauces, is prepared and cooked on board. It was common for American-based lines in particular to buy in some food from outside catering firms. This meant some of the equipment had not been used in many years and spare parts were required to bring it into use. The manufacturer was Hobart, but no one knew whether it had been purchased from Hobart UK, or Hobart US. To further complicate matters, parts numbers had changed over the years. Jo also commented on the great working relationship between departments. On one occasion, due to some illness on board, she had insufficient staff to man the Chocoholics Buffet – a highlight of any cruise and a chance for the pastry chefs to showcase their work. Her call for any available officers to help was swiftly answered and since many of them would not normally have any interaction with the passengers, they too enjoyed the occasion.

Crew barbeque on the stern of Deck One. This area is off limits to passengers.

Top left: Food & Beverage Manager Jo Haxby in her office, 13 June 2010. (*Andrew Sassoli-Walker*)

Above: The Chocoholics Buffet in the Coral Dining Room, 3 April 2009. This is a highlight of every cruise and is greatly looked forward to by passengers in need of that vital chocolate fix! It is usually combined with a tour of the galley.

Right: The Galley Status Board, 1 August 2010. This is an aid for kitchen staff, listing passenger numbers for each dinner sitting and timings for meals each day, as well as the night's Grill menu and Theme Buffet. The Grill is available (by reservation only) every evening in one half of the Conservatory. This allows passengers to dine in a more casual atmosphere than the Coral Dining Room. The other half of The Conservatory offers a different themed buffet every evening – seafood, Italian, Indian, etc. (*Andrew Sassoli-Walker*)

Above: An ice carving demonstration on deck. There is always one member of the Galley crew skilled in the art of carving fruit and ice into decorative shapes. It is amazing to watch these demonstrations on deck, when a large rectangular block of ice is shaped by saw, hammer and chisel into delicate animals and birds in a matter of minutes. (*Sharon Poole*)

Left: The atrium, decorated for Christmas 2005. (*Carlos Price*)

Right: Catering staff prepare for a deck barbeque at sea, May 2010. (*Sharon Poole*)

Below left: Gingerbread village in Tiffany's, Christmas 2005. This was made by the pastry chefs out of icing sugar, sweets and blue glazes (for the rivers). One is built on each P&O Cruises ship every Christmas. (*Carlos Price*)

Below right: Member of the deck crew varnishing the rails around the sun deck, May 2010. Maintenance of any ship is a never-ending task, exposed as they are to the worst the weather can throw at them. (*Sharon Poole*)

Left: Artemis arrives home at Southampton in the calm of a spring morning, 2008. (*Andrew Sassoli-Walker*)

Below left: Artemis seen at speed in the North Sea heading towards Norway in 2009, taken from the stern of *Aurora* by the author's (Andrew) father. (*Bob Walker*)

Below right: A powerful view of *Artemis* sailing down Southampton Water on one of her last season departures for P&O Cruises, 2010. (*Andrew Sassoli-Walker*)

Right: View from the foredeck looking aft towards the Bridge. In the foreground is the spare anchor. Anchors may be lost for many reasons. For example, on 20 May 2010, the Holland America Line's MS *Amsterdam* lost both her anchor and chain in the Harbour of Sitka, Alaska, when the braking system failed. (*Andrew Sassoli-Walker*)

Left: The ship's wake seen from the terrace aft of the Conservatory, May 2010. (*Sharon Poole*)

Above left: The Sun Deck, early morning, with the sun beds carefully arranged in neat rows, waiting for passengers to finish their breakfasts and choose their corner of the deck for the day. 8 May 2010. (*Sharon Poole*)

Above right: Artemis arriving in Southampton at sunrise in September 2008. This was the day the author (Andrew) embarked on his first cruise on the ship, while co-author Sharon was on board, sailing home from a twenty-four-night cruise to the Black Sea. (*Andrew Sassoli-Walker*)

Left: The distinctive tiered arrangement of stern decks that define *Artemis*. (*Andrew Sassoli-Walker*)

Opposite top: The tiered stern at sunset, as *Artemis* left the Solent to enter the English Channel at the start of a cruise to Northern European Cities, September 2008. (*Andrew Sassoli-Walker*)

Opposite bottom: The unmistakeable 1980s profile of the 'Little Ship with a Big Heart' as she was dubbed by Executive Purser Zak Coombs when he joined her in 2005. (*Andrew Sassoli-Walker*)

Passengers crowd onto the port side of *Artemis* as she leaves Southampton for a cruise to Norway and Iceland, 13 August 2010. The Captain (David Perkins) and pilot can be seen on the Bridge wing as the ship edges away from the dockside. (*Andrew Sassoli-Walker*)

Artemis in the Solent, 13 June 2010. The anchor in the foreground commemorates those brave soldiers and sailors that sailed from Lepe Beach in Hampshire in 1944 as part of Operation Overlord, more commonly known as D-Day. (*Andrew Sassoli-Walker*)

When Nicole Kennedy first joined the ship as Commercial Manager in charge of all the revenue-creating facilities (the Spa, Salon, shop, photographic shop, casino, tours desk, etc.) she said she was made very welcome and within a couple of weeks felt completely at home on board. Fewer crew and passengers mean her work is more hands-on with a personal approach. The ship can be completely restocked in two hours with between ten and twelve pallets of retail stock brought on board at Southampton on turn-around days.

Christine Noble has been Cruise Director on board for many years. While acknowledging the difficulties on occasion, with arranging sufficient variety of on-board events, given the limited number of public areas available on this size of ship, she also remarked on the wonderful sense of camaraderie among the ship's company. In the officer's dining room, there is one large table at which to sit, rather than lots of smaller tables. This encourages staff to mix more and any issues can be discussed over a meal, rather than in an official office visit.

To inform passengers of the contribution made to the smooth running of the ship by the many unseen workers, an '*Artemis* Uncovered' event is often held in the Atrium. Each department is represented – engineering, electro-technical, catering and so on – with photographs, equipment, tools, food and ingredients, and officers and crew members to explain what they all do. One such event, Zak Coombs recalled, was held on a formal night, and it was interesting to observe the contrast between the passengers heading into or out of the Coral Dining room in all their evening finery and the blue-overalled engineers who were responsible for all the luxuries that are taken for granted – running water, operating toilets, hot food, not to mention a moving ship!

CHAPTER 7

AND INTO THE FUTURE

In September 2009, P&O Cruises ended weeks of speculation when they announced that *Artemis* was in the process of being sold to the German company Phoenix Reisen. She was chartered back to P&O Cruises to complete her advertised programme, finishing with a special Farewell Cruise from 12 to 26 April 2011 to the Western Mediterranean. Then she will be renamed *Artania* and join a fleet of two other ships, *Albatros* and *Amadea*. Her present buff coloured funnel will be painted turquoise with the logo of the sun and an albatross added, and a similar coloured stripe will circle the hull. (N.B. The name of the ship is *Albatros* with one 's' as it is in German, but when referring to the logo, it has two!)

As *Artania* she will be based in the summer months in either Hamburg or Bremerhaven, and in the winter she will be operating cruises to the Mediterranean, Canary Islands and Madeira from Italy. For part of the winter she will sail for the South Atlantic and offer cruises round South America and the Falklands from either Buenos Aires or Valparaiso. It will herald a new chapter in the life of this beautiful ship which hopefully has many more years of service in her.

Southampton will still occasionally see her beautiful profile, as she is due to bring her German passengers to the UK as part of the Northern Europe itineraries.

The Phoenix Reisen website refers to the ship as 'MS *Artania* – elegant globetrotter with royal blood'. Praise indeed for a ship that in so many ways set the standard and helped the cruise industry offer what, today, we expect in terms of facilities and service.

Artemis will be replaced (rather confusingly) in the P&O Cruises fleet by the present *Royal Princess*, which will be renamed *Adonia*. This is one of the 35,000 ton R class ships – R8 – built for Renaissance Cruises in 2001. She will no doubt win many fans, but whether she will match the loyal following that *Artemis* achieved remains to be seen.

Farewell *Royal Princess / Artemis* and good luck in the latest chapter of your distinguished career.

An artist's impression of *Artemis* as she will look when she joins the fleet of German company Phoenix Reisen and is renamed *Artania*. (*Phoenix Reisen*)

APPENDICES

Firsts for *Royal Princess / Artemis*:

First ship to be built for Princess Cruises.

First and only modern cruise ship to have all outside cabins, every one of which has a large picture window or balcony.

First time the British £1 coin was used to lay in a dock under a new keel.

First to have computer accounting and a cashless on-board system.

First ship to have solid state radio transmitter/receiver equipment.

First ship to have an Electro Technical department.

First P&O ship to have a Computer Officer.

First ship to be completed at Wärtsilä's new £12 million fitting-out terminal in Helsinki.

First ship to have a live on-board TV channel showing passengers shipboard activities in the privacy of their cabins. This included, for example, a Bridge camera showing arrivals in ports or the transit of the Panama Canal.

First P&O ship to have an on-board fountain.

Held the first ever cruise-ship illusion show, specially put together by Cruise Director Rai Caluori and magician Michael Allport.

First ship to be christened at sea (as *Artemis*).

First female captain of a UK cruise ship.

Statistics & Information

Call Sign (as *Royal Princess*) GBRP; Port of registry London.

Call Sign (as *Artemis*) ZCDM7; Port of Registry Hamilton (Bermuda).

IMO Number 8201480

Gross Tonnage: 45,000

Length: 230 metres (757 feet)

Breadth: 32 metres (106 feet)

Draught: 8 metres (26 feet)

Service Speed: 20 knots

Maximum Speed: 22 knots

Artemis travels around 8 metres (26 feet) per litre of fuel at maximum speed.

Crew: 537

Regular Passenger Capacity: 1,200

Maximum Passenger Capacity: 1,260

Number of decks: Nine

130-150 tonnes of food stores are taken on board every turn-around day.

28 tonnes each of frozen food, fresh fruit and vegetables and bonded items (alcohol and tobacco) are consumed on a fourteen-night cruise.

1 ton of food is wasted on a fourteen-night cruise.

3,600 meals are prepared daily for passengers.

1,500 meals are prepared daily for the ship's company.

Around 3,000 photographs are taken every week.

1,000 miles of electric cable provides enough power to supply a town of 4,000 people.

ACKNOWLEDGEMENTS

The authors would like to thank everyone who has provided information, assistance and images for this book. In particular we would like to thank Captain Sarah Breton, the officers and crew of MV *Artemis*, April-August 2010, for the unfailing help, enthusiasm, access to the ship and time given to us over the duration of this project. Every effort has been made to obtain permission from the copyright owners of the photographs used, and we apologise if there are any omissions or errors.

We would also like to thank:
P&O Cruises, in particular, Philip Price and Charmaine Collins
The *Southern Daily Echo*
The *Weston & Somerset Mercury*
Commodore Bernard Warner, Master of *Queen Mary 2*
Lisa Galloway
Kerry McMaster
Pauline Sumsion

BIBLIOGRAPHY

100 Faces from Finland. A Biographical Kaleidoscope, Suomalaisen Kirjallisuuden Seura, 2000

Maxtone-Graham, John, *Liners to the Sun*, Sheridan House, 2000 ed.

McAuley, Rob, *The Liners – A Voyage of Discovery*, A Channel Four Publication, 1997

Peter, Bruce, *Knud E. Hansen A/S: Seven decades of ship design*, Forlaget Nautilus, Frederiksværk, Denmark, 2007

Quartermaine, Peter & Bruce Peter, *Cruise, Identity, Design & Culture*, Laurence King Publishing, 2006

Royal Princess, a Celebration, Sterling Publications Ltd, 1984

'The Great Liners – Southampton Ships Past & Present', *Southern Daily Echo*, 2009

Williams, David, *Glory Days of P&O*, Ian Allen Publishing, 1998

Artemis, rounding the Brambles Bank in the Solent, June 2010. (*Andrew Sassoli-Walker*)